Presented To

_____

From

_____

Date

_____

A
WEDDING
is a
FAMILY
AFFAIR

BRENDA HUNTER, PH.D.

A

WEDDING

is a

FAMILY

AFFAIR

KRISTEN BLAIR

A WEDDING IS A FAMILY AFFAIR
published by Multnomah Books
a part of the Questar publishing family

© 1995 by Brenda Hunter, Ph.D. and Kristen Blair

International Standard Book Number: 0-88070-836-0

Cover photo by Claudia Kunin

Cover design by David Carlson

Printed in the United States of America

Most Scripture quotations are from:
The New Revised Standard Version Bible (NRSV)
© 1989 by the Division of Christian Education
of the National Council of the Churches of Christ
in the United States of America

Also quoted:
The Holy Bible, New International Version (NIV)
© 1973, 1984 by International Bible Society,
used by permission of Zondervan Publishing House

New American Standard Bible (NASB)
© 1960, 1977 by the Lockman Foundation

For information:
QUESTAR PUBLISHERS, INC.
POST OFFICE BOX 1720
SISTERS, OREGON 97759

95 96 97 98 99 00 01 02 — 10 9 8 7 6 5 4 3 2 1

To Don,
the man who believed in me before
I believed in myself—
my husband, lover, friend.

Brenda

❦

To Greg,
the kindest man I've ever known.
Your wonderful heart and gracious spirit
have made the first year of marriage
the happiest of my life.

Kristen

CONTENTS

Chapter One

HOW DO I LOVE THEE?

How do I love thee? Let me count the ways.

I love thee to the depth and breadth and height

My soul can reach, when feeling out of sight

For the ends of Being and Ideal Grace.

ELIZABETH BARRETT BROWNING

SONNETS FROM THE PORTUGUESE

The doors swung open. As the organist played Lohengrin's "Bridal Chorus," the church resonated with sound. Was this real? Was I really getting married? This was a moment I'd imagined many times. I remembered twirling in pink tulle in my ballet classes, wondering what I would look like as a bride, and lying on my bed as a little girl, my chin resting in my hands, playing and replaying the moment when the doors would swing open, the audience would turn and stand, and I would glide down the aisle, resplendent in an elegant gown.... All those girlish dreams, all those expectations.

And now it was here. I was the bride, and at the end of that long aisle waited my groom, Greg. Dad and I began our measured march. I saw tender smiles, eyes glistening with tears, hands being held. Overwhelmed with the wonder of it all, I thought of the significance of the pledge I would soon make to Greg before God and His witnesses. So much drama, so many emotions woven into a few shining moments.

KRISTEN

At this moment you are probably still riding the crest of emotion you felt when you became engaged: euphoria, excitement, relief. The night Heather and John became engaged they couldn't wait to tell somebody their good news. So after John proposed, he and Heather hurried to her parents' townhouse. Once there, Heather announced what her parents had long suspected: "Guess what! John asked me to marry him!" Hugs and congratulations were exchanged all around before the engaged couple called John's parents, grandparents, and a few close friends—all before midnight. And when Heather finally returned home at two in the morning, her first priority was to carefully sculpt and paint her nails. Just in time, too, since her three roommates piled onto her bed at dawn the next morning to see her diamond.

In addition to euphoria, you probably feel profound relief that the search is finally over. The man of your fantasies and dreams has

❦

asked you to marry him. Jan, a thirty-three-year-old lawyer who lives in Raleigh, North Carolina, remembers her adrenaline high during the days after Rob proposed. "I thought, 'No more blind dates, no more singles groups, no more waiting for the right man to come along.'" Since men and women today are often older when they marry, this feeling of relief is genuine. Like many others, you may have already had several important relationships and even one or two failed romances. Just knowing the dating game is over has its own reward.

Love Has a Thousand Different Versions

Once you've shared your excitement with friends and family, your focus naturally turns to your upcoming wedding. Ah, the dreams of a wedding day. No doubt you have a vision of how you wish your day to unfold. You may want your dream wedding to occur in a garden surrounded by flowers, or in an old, historic church, or at home in front of a relaxed gathering of your family and closest friends. As seventeenth-century French moralist La Rochefoucauld wrote, "There is only one kind of love, but there are a thousand different versions."

For Peka Ann Wade and Walter A. Wilson III, their dream location was none other than a basketball court. Wilson, a city council member in Fairfax County, Virginia, and his bride, a title insurance agent, celebrated their two-and-a-half-minute ceremony and twenty-four-second toast at the George Mason University Patriot Center during the halftime of the Patriots and the New Hampshire Wildcats game.[1] Following their vows, the couple managed to cut the cake and squeeze in a dance to "Sea of Love" by the Honeydrippers before the basketball players thundered back onto the court. And, according to Jeff Riley, the assistant athletic director who helped with the ceremony, the couple got a "great round of applause."

Love's Labor

Whatever type of wedding you have in mind, you've probably just begun to realize the significance of the task at hand. Not only do you have myriad details to coordinate, but in a wedding—one of life's most glorious celebrations—you have to blend the longings, hopes, and expectations of two or more families.

What's it like to plan such a significant event? It's a bit like taking your first play to Broadway. All your encouragers, mentors, and supporters will be there to witness your debut. Excited, you realize you and your fiancé are novices and the stakes are high. Although you may have pictured your wedding day in your mind many, many times, you'll find the actual event is far different from anything you've imagined—more thrilling, and more stressful.

The Symbolism of Marriage

Why is a wedding so momentous and so complicated? The answer lies in all it symbolizes. For the friends and family members who come, your wedding is a time-honored event, a rite of passage. And for you and your fiancé, it's a public pledge of your love for each other for time and eternity. Once you marry, you cease to be two single adults and become instead a family. On the spiritual level, your wedding day is the time the two of you mystically become one. One flesh. Two souls fused together. While you have the rest of your lives to live out that oneness, the day you are pronounced husband and wife marks the beginning of your journey.

Although a wedding is heavy with symbolism, and you and your groom, along with your families, want yours to go well, how do you make this happen? How do you keep it from becoming one of those "nightmare" stories you've heard about? Here's one that takes the cake:

Dear Abby:

On the topic of disastrous weddings, mine ranks right up there at the top! While I was walking down the aisle, someone stepped on my train, ripping it from the back of my gown. My aunt immediately sprang from her seat yelling, "I'll fix it!" The wedding then ground to a halt while she tried unsuccessfully again and again to reattach it. I finally proceeded down the aisle with one hand behind me gripping my ripped train, and while ascending the steps to the altar—I fell!... At the conclusion of the ceremony, as we walked back up the aisle, the rabbi called out, "You forgot your bridal bouquet!"

...That's not all. When we arrived at our reception, the chef rolled out the cart bearing our gorgeous "wedding" cake. It was decorated with "Happy Birthday" and someone else's name on it.[2]

While wedding disasters do happen, they are rare. With careful planning, you can avoid nightmares at the same time you expect and accept some imperfections.

What most brides-to-be soon discover is that the greatest stress they experience comes from their close relationships. Why relationships? Many of the key players in your life and in your fiancé's life will have strong feelings and expectations about your wedding day. Trying to accommodate some of their expectations and also hold true to your own desires inevitably creates tension. You will find your communication and diplomacy skills stretched to the max in the months before your wedding. You will become the Henry Kissinger of negotiation, the Mother Teresa of compassion and understanding, the Napoleon Bonaparte of strategizing, and the Dave Barry of stress diffusion. Sound impossible? In a way it is. That is why you will need to stay focused on what's important to you and your fiancé, as well as those few items that are essential to your families.

A Wedding Is a Family Affair

Although in the first flush of engagement you and your fiancé have focused exclusively on each other, *your wedding is a family affair.* As you will soon discover, it conjures up profound emotions in your parents. Your father must now reckon with the fact that his little girl has grown up. Whether he has been close to you or not, he will likely struggle with profound feelings of loss. And your mother? Even if you and your mother are friends, the two of you may at times jockey for control over the wedding, prompting you to wonder "Whose wedding is it anyway?"

As you and your fiancé prepare for marriage, you'll find he has his own secret needs, hopes, and fears. It's important for you two to discuss *his* expectations for the wedding, the honeymoon, your life together.

And what about his parents? How can you start off on the right foot with them? After all, you are not just marrying a man, you are marrying into another family. How can you ensure they will see you as an asset rather than an intruder? What role will your fiancé's family play in planning the wedding so they don't feel invisible?

As for friends, some may react strongly to

your engagement. While some fear they will lose you as a confidante, others may be jealous you're marrying first.

Although most family members and friends will respond to your wedding positively, it's important to have a strategy for dealing with your supporters and detractors so you and your groom can celebrate your day of days.

And If Your Parents Are Divorced?

While healthy families are able to rally around an engaged couple to orchestrate a wedding with minimal stress, divorced and remarried parents often find this hard to do. Not surprisingly, parents who divorced because they couldn't get along may be daunted by the task of working together on something as intimate and challenging as a wedding. And many brides are anxious about planning such an important event with two people who are allergic to each other.

Eileen, a twenty-nine-year-old accountant who married several months ago, says, "The touchiest problem we faced was whether or not my dad would bring his girlfriend to our wedding. Since my parents had divorced only three months earlier, the pain was still fresh for all of us. I knew it would hurt Mom the most because she would be forced to meet Rita for the first time. In the end my fiancé and I suggested it would be better for Rita not to come. Dad reluctantly agreed but sulked throughout the ceremony. Why couldn't he focus on our day rather than his own agenda?"

Ah, the dilemmas posed by parental divorce. Since a wedding mirrors or magnifies existing family relationships—the distance, the closeness, the tensions—it's important to have a road map of the emotional terrain of your engagement. That's why we've written *A Wedding Is a Family Affair.* In this book you'll learn what to expect during the exhilarating months that lie ahead, including the psychological hurdles. While we have included some practical tips to help you prioritize and plan a timeline, we have focused primarily on feelings and emotions—yours, your fiancé's, your families'—to help you arrive at your wedding day a poised and radiant bride who feels supported by all those special people in her life. This book will also challenge you to look at the role of sex in your relationship with your fiancé and to create a strong spiritual foundation for your marriage.

This book is designed primarily for you to share with your fiancé, but you may also want to share chapters with your mother or other family members. Since your mother is a significant support player in this upcoming production, forging a strong alliance with her from the beginning will help both of you enjoy the experience with minimal conflict. As a mother-daughter team, we navigated many potential minefields in planning a recent, wonderful wedding, even with two blended families involved—proof that it's possible!

And we interviewed other brides, as well as mothers and fathers of brides, so you can hear different voices, like the following:

"When my daughter Shawn married a young farmer two years ago in a small but elegant ceremony, she decided to play a practical joke on her new husband. Before the reception she secretly changed shoes, and when he lifted her skirts to remove her garter, he found she was wearing farm boots!"—Patti Sparks, Indiana.

"As I was driving my daughter and her bridesmaids to the church, my daughter turned to me and said, 'Mom, sing the songs you used to sing as you tucked me into bed.'" —Jean Woody, Indiana

Each wedding has its funny, touching moments. So, let's plan your wedding together and celebrate the fact that your wedding is a family affair.

Chapter Two

YOUR GROOM: HIS SECRET NEEDS AND FEARS

If ever any beauty I did see, which I desired,

and got, 'twas but a dream of thee.

JOHN DONNE

FROM "THE GOOD-MORROW"

19

Friday, February 11, 1994. Because of the foul weather, Greg and I both had the day off—an opportunity to jump in the snow, listen to music, and talk. I wondered about the gorgeous floral arrangement he had hand-delivered earlier that day; it seemed strange to get flowers so close to Valentine's Day and my birthday. I also mused about our many conversations on marriage. As we climbed into the car to drive to dinner that evening, I couldn't help but eye Greg's pockets for any suspicious bulges where a ring might be concealed. Disappointed, I found none.

Once at the Chart House restaurant, we were soon seated at a window table and gazing outside, where ice chunks floated down the Potomac River. During dinner, Greg was unusually calm, confident, and talkative. As I listened to his soothing voice and watched his eyes, I wondered again why he had given me all those flowers. Was he telegraphing something? Suddenly Greg was on his knees in the deserted restaurant. "Will you marry me and

make me the happiest man in the world?" he asked. Then I saw the ring—a gorgeous, shimmering diamond. "Oh yes! Of course!" I replied, ecstatic. He took the ring and slipped it carefully on my finger. For a few moments we just sat and stared at its brilliance.

As we left the restaurant to walk along the river, Greg took my hand and started to sing "Dearly Beloved," an old song by Nancy Wilson that he had memorized just for this night: "Dearly beloved, how clearly I see, somewhere in heaven you were fashioned for me. Angel eyes knew you, angel voices led me to you. Nothing could save me, fate gave me a sign. I know that I'll be yours come shower or shine. So I say, merely, dearly beloved, be mine."[1]

KRISTEN

For a man, proposing marriage to the woman he loves is one of life's biggest moments, often causing him to go to great lengths to surprise and please her. Take Jerry Summers, for instance.

I met a wonderful lady when I was working out at the local gym three years ago.... Well, we'd been together for some time, and I finally decided to make my big move.... I thought, "Why don't I have myself gift-wrapped like a present and shipped to my girlfriend's place of work and propose in front of her whole company on Valentine's Day?"

...I spoke to the owner of A-1 Pack 'n' Ship, who found the story crazy but so heart-warming he agreed to do it.... I thought, what could top it off more than letting the whole world know how much I loved her? So I contacted the local television stations to see if they were interested in doing a special Valentine's Day story. Out of the five stations, one agreed and was thrilled with the idea. The station, Channel 2, also contacted the largest news-paper in Illinois to cover the story.

...We finally arrived at my girlfriend's office.... Chris's manager led her to the box and handed her the card she was to read aloud. The bottom of the card read: "I love you very much. Please open your present."

So she did and I popped out, got on my knees, and asked her to marry me. Everybody clapped and cheered while my girlfriend stood in amazement and cried with joy.... The planning took about three weeks, but it was all worth it.[2]

No less dramatic, Craig, a history teacher in Chesapeake, Virginia, rented a horse-drawn carriage and an Elizabethan costume, complete with pantaloons, a plumed hat, and cape to surprise his lady love. Joette had driven to Williamsburg that particular day with a girl-friend, and both were standing in front of the Williamsburg Inn when the carriage rolled by. Craig sprang out, fell to one knee, and asked Joette to marry him. How could she resist?

What Do Men Think of Marriage?

What causes a man to relinquish his free-wheeling ways and commit to one woman for life? Writer George Gilder says in *Man and Marriage* that a man finally settles down and makes a long-term commitment to marriage only because he has been "tamed." And the person who tames him? The woman he loves.[3]

Even after a man decides to marry, he experiences many of the same feelings a woman does—anticipation, hope, and no little apprehension. But gender differences do exist, and men have their private fears and longings regarding marriage.

According to Dr. Alvin Baraff, clinical psychologist and director of MenCenter Counseling, a man fears he will lose control of his home and life once he marries.[4] Will his new wife dictate how much time he spends watching sports on ESPN or how often he sees his male buddies? For a man, marriage signals the loss of independence, something he has enjoyed in great measure since childhood.

Baraff says, "It is important to remember that marriage is commonly an easier transition for women than men. Women have been taught emotional interdependence, sharing and closeness from a very early age. Young boys, on the other hand, are encouraged to be competitive, confrontational, and emotionally distant; in fact, emotional dependence of any kind is often seen as a weakness in a man."[5] Because of the vastly different ways men and women are raised in our culture, it's easy to understand why some men fear intimacy and commitment.

There's a Place for Space

Even so, men long for stable, fulfilling relationships just as women do, but they have different needs in relationships. How does this affect marriage? Drew says that before marrying Ellen he worried about a loss of "personal space." Ellen, like most women, loved to spend time talking and trying to understand Drew's thoughts and feelings. Although he enjoyed these times of intimacy, afterwards he usually needed time alone. "During our engagement I always knew I could go home to my own apartment and have time just to zone out, have total ownership of the remote control, watch sports—do what I wanted to do. With marriage, I worried about having some time when my mind could wander and I wasn't accountable to anyone." Because of Drew's concern, during their engagement he and Ellen talked about his need for personal space, and they worked on finding both the time and a place in their new home where each could be alone.

Is Drew's fear normal? In his book *Men Are from Mars, Women Are from Venus*, Dr. John Gray confirms that men need personal space and time apart from their mates. According to Dr. Gray, men respond to stress by going into their "caves."[6] This time, free from distractions and demands, helps a man regain his sense of self. So men move from intimacy to "cave-time" in a natural intimacy cycle. Dr. Gray cautions, "There are two ways a woman may unknowingly obstruct her male partner's natural intimacy cycle. They are: (1) chasing him when he pulls away; and (2) punishing him for pulling away."[7]

How can you accommodate your future husband's need for "cave-time" and thereby assure him that his needs matter to you?

❦ You can set aside an evening each week for solo activities—reading, listening to music, working on individual projects.

❦ Once you marry, you can create a room or space in your home that's his alone— a place to retreat and read, watch television, or listen to music. Don't get angry if he needs an hour at the end or beginning of the day that's just his.

❦ Encourage the continued development of personal interests, whether it means taking classes, having a weekly men's group, playing baseball or basketball. Too much togetherness makes us grow stale and flat.

Other Fears of Marriage

In addition to the fear of losing personal space, most men have performance anxiety— in several arenas. Men in our society are

23

reared to perform—athletically, academically, and economically. From the time they are little boys, they perform under their father's watchful eye. And their mother's. Because of their need for parental love and approval, they are primed to look for feedback. Sometimes they get love and affirmation; sometimes they get painful criticism.

Syndicated columnist Mike Harden writes about his relationship with a critical father, who tried to spur his performance by calling him a "pantywaist."[8] Whether Mike played ball with his dad as a nine-year-old or sat through his taunts as a teenager, he longed to measure up to his dad's expectations. He writes, "Few sons truly understand their fathers. We thrash and founder just below the tide of paternal expectation, suffocating in self-doubt, clawing for adulation. As children, we avenge the sting of criticism, the absence of praise, in fantasy. We imagine ourselves the sons of more appreciative fathers."[9]

Not only do sons grow up wanting to be heroes in their father's eyes—a status often grounded in performance—but this need to excel, to be okay, extends to their relationships with their wives, in the sexual arena in particular. One groom, a thirty-year-old bank manager, admitted, "I wonder if I will be able to please my wife sexually. Will I be able to perform in bed?" This fear is particularly strong for men who have abstained sexually.

What can you do to relieve your fiancé's performance anxiety? Get him to talk about his fears and listen to his heart. Your reassurance will be a powerful antidote to his worries. But be sure to share your own anxieties as well. This will help him realize you're in this together, that sex is a shared experience, not a one-man show. Playfulness and humor help greatly. Couples who play together and diffuse situations with laughter are able to establish lifelong patterns that enhance their sexual relationship.

Along with their insecurities about control, personal space, and sexual performance, many men also worry about being accepted by their fiancée's family. They want to be seen

Not only do sons grow up wanting to be heroes in their father's eyes...but this need to excel, to be okay, extends to their relationships with their wives.

❦

as a good marital choice. Larry, who recently married, says, "When I met Sally's family, I was wondering, do they really like me? Do they think I'm a good person?" Fortunately he did feel accepted by her parents and siblings. "The fact that Sally's family liked and approved of me," says Larry, "helped a great deal in my transition to marriage."

Men also fear a change in their friendships with their buddies. Bill, a new husband, says, "In a sense, when I married, I lost something with my friends. I lost the spontaneity and primary position I had in my buddies' lives. No matter how close we were before marriage, now there's someone else who always carries more weight in my life." When they marry, men exchange spontaneity in their friendships

for more predictability and stability. And even if they see this as necessary and important, they will probably have some difficulty adjusting initially.

What else is your future husband likely to fear? In talking to grooms, we found these to be their most frequent concerns:

❦ Will my wife be faithful?

❦ Will my feelings of love for her change? What if I fall out of love? Do we truly understand what love is?

❦ Will my wife take care of herself—her looks and her health—once we marry? Will she gain weight?

❦ Will she nag me or talk me to death?

❦ Will she opt for a divorce if the going gets tough?

Since deep and revealing communication is essential for a satisfying marriage, it's important that you encourage your fiancé to discuss his feelings with you. Listen without being defensive. Understand that his concerns are to be expected, and try to deal with each one. He will appreciate your empathy and love you for understanding. And if he's not a particularly articulate guy? Practice patience, and try to help him express his feelings as best he can.

Your Fiancé's Needs

In addition to his fears, your fiancé has certain needs, which he may or may not be able to express. One groom we interviewed said one of his most important needs was the companionship his future wife offered. Although he has numerous male buddies, Joe believes women are better able to help men become vulnerable. "They're not into the male, macho stuff," he says. "I can let down my guard with my fiancée in a way I never could with the guys."

Your future husband needs your encouragement as well as your companionship. He longs for your approval, your affirmation, your life-giving, positive words. He may or may not have received the praise he needed growing up, but now he has a chance to bask in your love and admiration. As a result of his fiancée's affirmation, Jay, an aerospace engineer, feels he gained greater confidence at work during the nine months prior to his wedding. "Because Laura believed in me and encouraged me to take risks, I became more vocal," he says. "Instead of just sitting in meetings and thinking about what the program needed, I began to speak up. And my newfound assertiveness was rewarded after our marriage with a much larger raise."

Just as you need the stability and promise that marriage affords, so does your groom. Tired of dating, he's ready to commit and enjoy the permanence of marriage. Dr. Baraff believes that men, like women, have a biological clock that tells them it's time to think of wife, home, and children. For some, the clock ticks in their twenties. For others, this clock ticks loudly in their thirties, when they begin to long for the married life.[10] Then a man understands as perhaps never before that he needs someone he can count on for picnics, sunsets, vacations, each day's special moments, and family life.

In addition, your future husband needs you to value the role marriage will confer on him: husband and provider. Unless he has been previously married, he has had to take care of only himself since his emancipation from his family. Once married, he can flex and grow. He is now able to mature in ways only marriage can afford. He can now become a good family man, the provider for his family.

Never underestimate the good feelings a man gets from being a provider, even if his wife is also employed. Despite thirty years of feminism, "Men themselves speak clearly of how important it is to their sense of self to provide well for their families."[11] Psychologist Faye Crosby, author of *Juggling,* found in her research that men carry an image of family in their minds throughout the workday. In their minds, they work not just "for their own glory" but for their families as well.[12]

Steve admits that his engagement to Lisa had a big impact on his feelings about his job. "Before Lisa and I got engaged, work was more about me. Because I was working just to support myself, I was self-focused. But after we became engaged, a real shift took place. I became more aware of my role as a provider and began to ask myself, 'How stable is this job?' I wanted to be on a path that would provide a good income for Lisa and our future family."

A couple who recognizes these fears and desires and addresses them during the engagement period starts off their marriage on a more secure footing. But what about the wedding itself? How involved do grooms get? Couples who are older and have been on their own for quite some time may plan their wedding without much parental input. In fact, they may choose to fund the wedding themselves and be solely responsible for all decisions. On the other hand, if the bride is younger, her mother may assume a major role.

If this is the case, the mother of the bride needs to acknowledge that the groom's wishes, along with the bride's, matter most. Otherwise, the groom may feel discouraged from participating. Initially Mike was eager to help Julie with all aspects of planning their wedding. Since Julie was stressed as she completed her final year of medical school, Mike headed out with her mother to look for reception sites for their May wedding. Unfortunately Julie's mother was unresponsive to most of Mike's suggestions, leaving him feeling frustrated and helpless. As a result, he grew silent and withdrew. On the other hand, Dave's future mother-in-law provided suggestions and input but allowed Dave and Amy to make the final decisions. Dave remarked, "Sure, we had to make concessions to Amy's parents, but I was a major player in the decisions."

Finally, enjoy having your groom plan the honeymoon. Often a bride, exhausted by all the wedding plans, is relieved to have her fiancé take care of the honeymoon. Carol gave her fiancé, Tim, free rein in planning their time away. Her only specifications? "I wanted to go to a beach, somewhere warm, somewhere Tim had never been before, so we could discover it together." Lisa took a similar route. "I gave John the total responsibility for planning our honeymoon. I simply told him I wanted our honeymoon to be stress free." As it turned out, the men took their cues and made great choices: Carol and Tim flew to Bermuda, and John planned a relaxing trip to Scotland for Lisa.

Changing Priorities

As your groom moves closer to marriage, he realizes he must change his priorities. In becoming your husband he must separate psychologically from his own family and become the head of a new family. The engagement period is a natural time to begin the separation process, as the two of you consult each other first and allow your individual concerns to take precedence over parental concerns. However, your fiancé may have difficulty going against what he has naturally learned to do over his lifetime. And it will take time for him to become accustomed to deferring to you, his fiancée and future wife, before all others. If he struggles to put you ahead of family loyalty, be patient. This strong loyalty which binds him to parents and siblings will soon be transferred to you.

Having a mentor will help your fiancé with the changes an engagement and marriage require. If he is close to his dad, this is a great time for them to work around the house or go sailing, and talk, talk, talk. If not, he may want to find an older man, perhaps one in his church or at work, who can advise him about the pressures and changes he's facing. In addition, it would be advantageous for your father to talk with him. Not only would this help integrate your fiancé into your family, but it would, no doubt, please your father as well. Since you are inundated with wedding details, you may not be able to fully appreciate the cataclysmic changes in your fiancé's life. But another man, particularly one who is married and communicative, can address these concerns from the male perspective and put your groom at ease.

Just remember that *both* of you are in transition and *both* of you have fears and concerns. That's why you can profit from conversations with mentors. Talk to one another, but also seek out those who are a few steps ahead. These people—parents, friends or an older couple—can encourage you as you march toward your wedding day. As a result, you will feel reassured, confident that you are on track for a satisfying life together.

A Final Note

Above all, keep a sense of humor and enjoy the process of growing closer. And remember, mishaps can become some of your fondest memories. Here's one of our favorite groom stories:

So conscientious was the groom that he arrived early to inspect the arrangements at the New York synagogue and make sure everything was set up as planned. About a half-hour before the service was to begin, he went into a back room to change into his tuxedo—and realized he had been so busy attending to details that he had forgotten it! The organist noticed that while the ceremony was scheduled to begin any minute, the groom was helplessly pacing the floor in jeans and a sweatshirt. He approached the young man, who explained the situation. The organist immediately offered his own tuxedo. The screen set up around the organ made for a makeshift changing room, and the groom slipped into the borrowed clothing and ran to meet his bride. Still hidden from sight, the generous organist commenced his playing of the "Wedding March"—in his underwear.[13]

Chapter Three

WHOSE WEDDING IS
IT ANYWAY?

Thou art thy mother's glass, and she in thee

Calls back the lovely April of her prime.

SHAKESPEARE

"SONNET III"

How well Susan Yates, author of *A House of Friends,* remembers the day she and her daughter Allison went looking for the wedding dress. Since she and Allison, a senior at the University of Virginia, were working with a tight budget, Allison had already pursued the secondhand route, trying on her mother's, grandmother's, and even a friend's wedding dresses. Unfortunately nothing looked good or fit.

So one day in late winter Susan and Allison, along with a troupe of friends, sisters, and cousins drove to a bridal shop owned by a German dressmaker. Upon arriving, they climbed the stairs to the dressing rooms above, and Allison began her search. After trying on one elegant gown after another, she finally found one that she and everyone else loved. Since the style had been discontinued, the dress was on sale and the price was affordable. The only hitch? Allison couldn't return the dress should she change her mind.

With no little anxiety Allison purchased the dress, and the group piled into their cars and headed homeward. Once there, Susan took her husband, John, and his friend Bob aside and said conspiratorially, "In a few minutes Allison's going to try on her dress for you. No matter what you think, RAVE! Her confidence is a little shaky right now."

While the men waited expectantly in the family room, upstairs the women decided to have a little fun. One of Allison's sisters had received a secondhand Rose from Japan with layers of faded sequins and bouffant sleeves—reminiscent of a sixties prom dress. Instead of her lovely wedding gown, Allison donned the faded dress and sallied into the room where the men waited expectantly.

As if on cue, they gushed, "What a beautiful dress!" John was especially effusive. Then his friend Bob picked up the chorus, dripping compliments about how wonderful Allison looked. Finally Allison's father, who knew the women in the family only too well, paused and said quietly, "No, that's not the dress," at which point all the women dissolved in laughter. Later when Allison tried on her real wedding gown, her father and mother smiled their approval. As she twirled round and round for all to see, she looked like what she would soon become—a happy and radiant bride.

The Most Complex Relationship in the Family

Mothers and daughters. This most complex relationship in the family system comes into sharp focus at the time of a daughter's wedding. A daughter looks to her mother not only as her bridal consultant and implementer of her dreams but also as a steady encourager and friend. And both probably long for those warm, rich "bonding" experiences that folklore says is theirs for the asking.

Certainly buying the wedding gown is for many mothers and daughters a memorable, happy time. As we look back over the months leading up to the wedding, the day we went questing for the dress stands out in bold relief as our special day. We were close, united— two women with a common goal. And at the end of the day, after we had purchased the elegant gown with its bodice of Belgian lace, we met the men in our lives at a restaurant on the Potomac River to celebrate.

As you think about purchasing your wedding dress, plan a special day with your mother. Of course, you two may shop for weeks for the perfect gown, but even so enjoy this experience as a memorable time, something you can look back on with warmth and joy.

In the days ahead you'll discover you need your mother more than you have in years, not only for her practical help but also for her emotional support. After all, for many of you your mom has been your primary comforter and cheerleader. And a wedding is a high-stress time when you will need her comforting presence and expertise in spades. She's your friend—and a key player in realizing your wedding dreams.

While your father may be privately lamenting the loss of his little girl, your mother knows she has an important and complex job to do—helping you plan and orchestrate your

In the days ahead you'll discover you need your mother more than you have in years, not only for her practical help but also for her emotional support.

❧

wedding. For this reason, the time with your mother prior to your wedding will be filled with more constructive, goal-oriented, planning sessions. You and your dad may opt for warm, emotional moments as he strives to let go, but your mother will probably deal with her emotions much later in the process—once the wedding planning is complete and the last few days are upon her. That's when many mothers are surprised by the intensity of their emotions.

"I haven't slept soundly for years," says Karen, "so I found myself awake around three o'clock one morning that last week before Laurie's wedding. I had been so busy that only then did I feel the sadness her wedding inspired. After all, my baby was leaving home forever. I cried, read, prayed, and felt better. Because

I had felt that sadness, when her wedding day came, I was excited and happy."

Shared Roles

Your mother may realize that in this next stage of your life you two will have more in common than ever before. While you may have spent your twenties or even thirties separating from her and forging your identity, once you become a wife, you have a new relationship. No longer simply mother and daughter, you are now adult women and wives. Your mother, you will discover, has much to teach you. And should you become a mother yourself, your relationship will take an even deeper turn. So while your dad may be lost in his private sadness just now, your mother perhaps anticipates the prospect of growing even closer to you once you marry. That's why she concentrates on the business at hand and sorts out her emotions either late at night or over lunch with her best friend.

But to the business at hand. As you two begin to sort out the guest list, choose a reception site, and think about photographers and flowers, some stresses and tensions in your relationship are inevitable. So how can you two make it through the rapids without capsizing your raft?

A Look at the Mother-Daughter Bond

The relationship a bride-to-be has had with her mother since childhood will be reflected in the wedding planning experience itself. Some women have warm, positive relationships with their mothers complete with healthy boundaries and tons of mutual respect.

Women who feel secure in their mothers' love and acceptance sail through their teens into their free-form twenties, able to speak their minds honestly and take risks. For these brides, sharing hours and days with their mothers pouring over wedding manuals and dealing with service personnel will be, for the most part, a positive, heart-warming experience. Sure, they will have taxing moments and flared tempers when superstressed. But the mother who has been her daughter's encourager, confidante, and friend will focus more on the younger woman's feelings and desires than on planning the social event of the season.

For those who have a distant or even conflictual relationship with Mom, planning a wedding causes old tensions and feelings to resurface. Unless a relationship is reworked, old patterns will continue to come into play. Take Gina and Rachel, for instance.

Gina glanced at her watch nervously. She had been engaged to Tom for just two weeks when she and her mother planned this "women only" meeting with great excitement and a little apprehension. Strong-minded women, they had often disagreed in the past.

When Rachel, her mother, arrived, the two women chose a corner table and began chatting amicably. Soon Rachel sat back in her chair and asked her daughter, "What kind of wedding do you and Tom plan to have?" As she listened to her daughter talk about getting married in a new, nondenominational church rather than the old, prestigious family church, Rachel felt her anxiety rising. "It just doesn't make sense. Why don't you and Tom get married in our church, especially since your father and I will host the wedding?" Gina patiently explained her position. Appearing to listen, her mother continued to press for what she wanted. Finally Gina stood up, flung her napkin on the table, and declared, "It's my wedding, Mother. Mine and Tom's. We can get married anywhere we want." Gina left the restaurant hastily, just as she used to race to her room and slam the door as a child when she felt her mother was intractable.

Later that evening Rachel returned home, discouraged and depressed, and told her husband about the conversation. A veteran of numerous female wars, he sighed, "And this is only the beginning."

Control. Territoriality. These are big issues for some brides and their mothers once the euphoria fades and the real work of planning a wedding begins. Within days some mothers and daughters begin to draw lines in the sand. After all, each woman has her own list of priorities, her own ideas about where a reception should be held, and how extensive the guest list should be. Before long, the negotiations begin in earnest.

Why Are Some Mothers Controlling?

Like Gina and Rachel, some mother-daughter pairs have a history of jockeying for control over everything from makeup, to boyfriends and curfews. In these instances the mother holds on too tightly, and the daughter feels her wishes aren't heard or respected. What's behind this jockeying for control?

At base, a mother may feel insecure. She may fear that the thread of mother love will be slowly pulled out of her hands. She is, after all, preparing to share her daughter with a new and possibly unknown family. From this point on her daughter will have to accommodate another family's needs and schedules during holidays and birthdays. As a mother, she will have to stand back and allow her daughter to love another woman. For some mothers this is a threatening experience, particularly if they are insecure in their daughter's love. And even if they aren't, the prospect of having one's daughter acquire another mother creates anxiety.

Sally Friedman, writing in *Bride's* magazine, addresses this issue head-on. She viewed Ruth, her daughter's future mother-in-law, as a threat.[1] "She is accomplished, sensitive, altogether charming, and unspeakably thin," writes Sally. "It's no wonder that I automatically and reflexively resented her when she first came into my life. Or, should I say, into Nancy's life." Already anxious about sharing her "beloved Nancy" with another mother, Sally was jealous of Nancy's special camaraderie with her future mother-in-law. In fact, Nancy spoke admiringly of Ruth's "perfectly cut black hair, her megawatt smile, her luminous skin."

Only as Sally got to know Ruth, not as a competitor for her daughter's love but as a new friend, did she begin to relax and feel more secure. It helped when Sally realized she and Ruth had something powerful in common: their genuine love for their children. "We are mothers who love our children beyond all reason,"[2] Sally writes. Recognizing this, she was finally able to link arms with Ruth as support players for their children's new family.

But there are other reasons a mother may be controlling. Since the bride's parents usually fund and host the wedding, a mother probably feels she has a powerful and pivotal role in the planning process. And, in truth, she does. Traditionally she has not only overseen myriad details but has borne the responsibility for seeing that everything goes according to plan. Also, mothers who are sensitive to social approval may feel they will be evaluated by prescribed patterns of decorum and etiquette. Other mothers simply admit that they are, and have long been, control freaks.

When to Hold, When to Fold, and Other Strategies for Dealing with Mom

Even if you understand some of the reasons for your mother's behavior, how can you better negotiate with her? Where do you draw the line between being compliant and setting boundaries?

When Jeannie announced her engagement, her father came to her in private and said, "Honey, you know we'd have a lot less tension around here if you'd just go along with your mother." A recent college graduate, Jeannie agreed, so her mother planned the wedding she wanted her daughter to have.

While Jeannie was content with the arrangement then, now, years later, she admits, "I wish our wedding had had a stronger spiritual emphasis. But at the time I just wanted to get married, and I was too immature to press for what I wanted."

While Jeannie was willing for her mother to "give" her a wedding, Cynthia was not. She knew from the beginning she wanted to be the woman at the helm. "I was thirty, had a good job, and had a mortgage on an apartment, for goodness' sake. I wasn't going to let my mother plan my wedding. So my fiancé and I decided exactly what we wanted her to do. Thankfully, she was willing to go along with our plans."

If a bride is older, it is generally easier for her to take charge of her wedding from the outset—her mother may be used to being a support player rather than a director. Amy Tomko, who married at thirty-two, diplomatically asked her mother to help with specific tasks, like flower selection. "I knew what I wanted," says Amy, "and I was able to convince my mother that what I was asking for was reasonable." Amy found that the tensions were reduced and the two women got along because she defined her mother's responsibilities early on.

Whether you and your mom are best friends or not, whether you are twenty or thirty, it's important that your parents feel their ideas and suggestions are respected—and in some cases followed. Parents who are funding a wedding will likely have some non-negotiables. Tucker Vicellio says her husband had only one nonnegotiable for his two daughters' weddings: he didn't want to pay for a disc jockey. "He just didn't like them," says Tucker, "but he was willing to pay for a small band." So when daughter Catherine married at twenty-four, the Vicellios hired a Dixie Land band, and the bride's father was happy.

To determine your family's nonnegotiables, discuss your plans with your parents, and listen to their desires. Be willing to bend on their key issues, particularly if they are funding a large part of the wedding. In addition to nonnegotiables, your mother may feel

strongly about certain areas. If you don't have definite opinions in these instances, why not consider these potential areas for compromise? Elisabeth remembers that she and her mother had markedly different ideas about wedding dresses. Their solution? Elisabeth chose the dress, while her mother selected an appropriate veil. Ann, a thirty-eight-year-old bride, had definite ideas about the kind of wedding she wanted, but she also wanted to honor her mother. So she decided to ask her mother to be the first to look at the reception site with her, and she agreed to have one of her mother's friends supply the flowers.

You may even consider letting your mother follow through on an idea you think is illogical or impractical. "My mother wanted an ice sculpture at my wedding reception," says Kelly, a thirty-year-old press secretary. "Although I didn't think it was a good idea, I let her pursue it. Mom eventually came to see it was an unnecessary expense. In the process we avoided a battle." By figuring out your priorities and nonnegotiables, you and your groom

A daughter looks to her mother not only as her bridal consultant and implementer of her dreams but also as a steady encourager and friend.

❦

will soon learn when to stand firm and when to compromise. Remember that familiar adage: "Pick the mountains you die on."

Mothers Aren't Perfect, But Neither Are Weddings: So Focus on Your Relationship

You and your mother can greatly reduce the tension in the planning process if you agree on one essential: good feelings are worth preserving. When Susan Yates and her daughter Allison began to plan Allison and Will's wedding, Susan told her, "I want this experience to be fun. I've never been a mother of the bride before, so I will make mistakes. But I want you and Will to tell me if I step on any toes. What's key here are the relationships, not the event itself."

Whether your mother is a novice at planning a wedding or an old pro, it's vital that you and she focus on your relationship rather than the "perfect wedding." After all, no such event exists. Once you accept this, your expectations become more realistic and you'll feel less stress. And if both you and your mother emphasize your relationship rather than the wedding itself, the issue of control recedes into the background. What helps? Ask each other frequently, "How's it going?" or "How are you handling all this wedding stress?" Then try to listen to each other's response without anger or defensiveness.

And if you and your mother find yourselves

too often angry at each other? Why not get help. Talk to a trusted friend or counselor, and use what you've learned about yourself and this relationship to advantage. Since your relationship with your mother is central your whole life long, it's important that you emerge from this time stronger friends, if at all possible.

The Invisible Mother

While some brides struggle with strong-minded and controlling moms, others have a different dilemma: the invisible mother. Although Tracy has been married for several years now, she remembers with sadness that her mother, who lived only four hours away, was too busy with her own life to help her shop for a wedding gown. Fortunately Tracy's best friend, Sara, stepped in and gave much needed support and encouragement. But that didn't dissipate Tracy's pain. "My mother simply refused to do very much," says Tracy. "It hurt then and it still hurts. Mom said that since her own mother was domineering, she was determined to give me all the freedom and personal space I needed. I just wish she had asked me what I wanted." Tracy's need for support collided with her mother's determination not to repeat her own mother's mistake. Since Tracy's mother had not confronted her own pain, she unwittingly inflicted pain on her daughter, just as her mother had done to her years before.

Sometimes mothers are not as involved as their daughters wish because of physical rather than psychological distance. So what's a mother to do when she lives in another state or across the country? She may not be able to be a "hands-on" planner, but her advice and counsel still carry a lot of weight, and her encouragement and support become even more important during phone conversations and occasional visits.

When a Mother Is Divorced

What happens when a mother is divorced? Life gets even more complicated. Cindy, whose mother never remarried, remembers that planning her wedding was extremely delicate. "My mother was so negative about marriage she couldn't get excited about mine," she admits wistfully. Another bride, Diane, was the youngest of five children and the last to leave home. Since her mother never remarried after her divorce, having her "baby" leave meant she was truly alone. Diane felt torn. She understood her mother's sadness, but she was, nevertheless, eager to start her new life. And because she was acutely aware of her mother's feelings, she felt somewhat cheated. She longed for her mother to share her joy, but instead she felt pulled into taking care of her mother emotionally.

Let's face it. For many divorced mothers the prospect of a daughter's wedding conjures up mixed emotions. On the one hand, they're happy their daughter has met the man she loves; on the other, they may have difficulty believing their daughter's marriage will last. After all, theirs didn't. While there's no way to instantly change a mother's view, a daughter can affirm her commitment to a lasting marriage, while emphasizing the importance of their mother-daughter relationship and the unchallenged place her mother will always have in her heart.

But it's not a daughter's job to be her mother's emotional caretaker, either in childhood or adulthood. And if a daughter assumed that role growing up or at the time of the divorce, now is the time to begin to set healthy boundaries. She can encourage her mother to turn to friends, a support group, a minister, or a counselor for help with her ambivalence or residual pain from divorce. What's central is that each woman has a supportive network so she can air her frustrations in private and not overload the mother-daughter relationship at this all important time.

A Mother Relives Her Wedding When Her Daughter Marries

Since a mother sees herself in the "mirror" of her daughter, most mothers of the bride find themselves reminiscing when a daughter prepares to marry. In fact, a mother may try to provide her daughter with something that was missing from her own experience. Maria, a high-powered executive in New York, is already thinking about her daughters' future weddings even though they are still children. When Maria married fifteen years ago, she wanted a beautiful, four-hundred-dollar gown. She raved about the dress to her stepmother, who refused to buy it, saying the dress was too expensive. So Maria halfheartedly found another dress at half the price. Today Maria says sadly, "Money wasn't the issue. My stepmother just didn't love me enough. When my daughters marry, the sky's the limit. I won't do to them what my stepmother did to me." Pausing, she reflects, "You know, you can never really do a wedding over again."

Is it healthy for a mother to try to heal herself as her daughter marries? A daughter's wedding can provide an opportunity for some inner healing, but a mother needs to understand how her past experiences affect her so she doesn't spend her family into debt or end up hurting her daughter's feelings. We dealt with this "ghost of weddings past" and emerged winners.

It became clear something was going on when Kristen and I had our third argument about the size of the guest list. Although my husband and I were paying for the reception, Kristen was the designated wedding comptroller, and she wanted to come in well below budget for her wedding luncheon. While she preferred to invite fewer people, I was adamant about having enough people attend her wedding. Sparks flew; we argued vehemently until I slowly understood why I felt so strongly about having a longer guest list.

I remembered a painful scene from my own first wedding, a traditional affair similar to the one Kristen was planning. As I stood waiting for the doors of the southern Presbyterian church to swing open, the six-year-old flower

43

girl, Ruthie, peeked through the crack in the door and said, "Where are all the people? I was in another wedding last week and the church was full." Had I been a confident young woman, I would have ignored her comment. As it was, I felt stricken. My fiancé and I had planned our wedding from college dorms with little parental involvement. Even though we had just graduated from college, we had paid for a lot of our own expenses. I had paid a seamstress to make a dress from my earnings. And as we sent out our invitations, we assumed all our friends and relatives would come. How vulnerable I felt as I became acutely aware of those who were missing.

In remembering this I suddenly understood what was driving me: I didn't want Kristen's experience to mimic mine, nor did I want to feel those painful emotions a second time. When I was finally able to express this to Kristen, the tension between us evaporated. She, in turn, shared her realistic concerns about money, and we were able to compromise. Both of us agreed to stick to the wedding budget she

and Greg had designated, and if more people came than we had estimated, Don and I would happily absorb the extra cost.

BRENDA

So if you find yourself locked in an intense power struggle with your mother, try to discover what's going on beneath the surface. Ask her to tell you about *her* wedding—its tensions, struggles, and joys. Not only will you learn a lot, but you may be able to understand how her past is affecting both of you in the present. As you become aware of the emotions your wedding engenders in your mother, you'll better understand why she feels so intensely about certain things. And if she will listen to your concerns, the two of you can find a happy, win-win solution.

The Last Hurrah

As you and your mother work together, don't forget to be open to serendipitous moments. Sometimes, like the search for a wedding gown, they are planned. At other times they occur unexpectedly, especially in those last few days before your wedding. And when they occur, you will find that you are caught up in moments of deep joy.

The Thursday night before Kristen's Saturday morning wedding I couldn't sleep. So I got out of bed, left my snoring husband, and pulled the door shut behind me. Moments later I gently pushed open Kristen's bedroom door and heard her quietly call out to me, "Mom, is that you?"

"I can't sleep."

"I can't either," she said.

So just as I had done many nights when she was a little girl, I lay down on my daughter's bed beside her and stroked her hair. During her childhood, Kris had loved this daily bedtime ritual when, in the dark, she could relax and pour out her heart.

"Mom, I'm anxious," she said.

"About sex?"

"No, I'm worried about sharing toothpaste. About sharing personal space."

I laughed, enjoying her response. And then my mind shifted gears. "Do you remember when you were three years old and we lived in England? I can still see you with your navy plaid jumper, your blue tights covering your chubby little legs, and those black Mary Jane's. Your hair was so fine; I kept it short and it looked like chicken feathers."

"Yeah, I remember skipping down the street, holding your hand on those mornings after we had taken Holly to school."

And we were off, tripping down memory lane, wrapping up the first twenty-five years of my younger daughter's life, our sleepy voices back and forth in the dark.

Soon I rose to leave, and as I opened the door, I turned and spoke into the silky darkness, "You'll be a beautiful, regal bride in just two days, Krissy, but you'll always be my baby."

BRENDA

Chapter Four

THE FATHER OF THE BRIDE

So are you to my thoughts as food to life,

Or as sweet-seasoned showers are to the ground.

SHAKESPEARE

"SONNET LXXV"

If you haven't already, you will likely soon watch *Father of the Bride,* a tender movie starring Steve Martin and Diane Keaton. A remake of an earlier version featuring Elizabeth Taylor and Spencer Tracy, this film captures the powerful connection between a father and daughter—a bond that stirs up intense feelings of love and loss in a father's heart as his daughter marries. One scene in particular reveals the father's struggle.

As the Banks family sits around the dinner table, daughter Annie, recently returned from months of study abroad, struggles to tell her family about the man she has met in Rome—and is planning to marry. Incredulous, her father looks across the table at his daughter, but in place of a twenty-two-year-old woman, he sees and hears a child in pigtails announce, "Daddy, we're going to get married." George Banks's response? He simply can't believe his little girl would do such a thing. She is, after all, too young. His wife, Nina, reminds him that she was a mother when she was twenty-two. George then tries a different tack. He asks what the young man does for a living. "Independent communications consultant? Does that mean he's unemployed?" George responds.

While Nina and Annie patiently work with George, the audience laughs. We realize we are witnessing a father caught in the throes of powerful emotions as he struggles to let his daughter go. How could his only daughter, who has always adored him, even conceive of giving all that love and adoration to another man? Leave her father? Unthinkable.

George and Annie have a ritual that encapsulates their relationship—playing basketball together. Annie, who is as skilled at scoring points as her father, dances after each basket she lands. And on the eve of her wedding when she can't sleep, Annie plays in the driveway, shooting baskets solo, symbolizing that she's leaving an era and her father behind. Later her dad comes out and joins her, and together they play their final game as father and child.

If you and your father are close, perhaps you also have shared a special activity over the years. If so, now is the time to schedule some of those moments. Play tennis or golf together. Or spend a day fishing. Even if you have few shared activities, plan lunches out, or a day of hiking, or even working in the yard together since men communicate around activities. As you're together, ask your dad how he feels about your wedding. Although most men have a harder time communicating their feelings than women do, some will open up. After all, a wedding is one of life's most emotional moments. This is a good time for you to listen to your dad with your heart.

Debbie and her dad enjoyed a last lunch out several days before her June wedding. "I've always loved having lunch alone with my dad," says Debbie. "He's a wonderful listener and hangs on my every word. So it was natural to want to spend time with him the week before the wedding. But this time I asked him how he felt, and he almost cried. He told me I would always be his little girl and he wanted me to have a good life. At that, I began to cry. It was a sweet, tender moment."

Your wedding is a bittersweet time for your father. You can help by giving him the opportunity to talk about his feelings. It will definitely be harder for him to let you go than it will be for you to leave. After all, you're leaving home for a whole new life with the man you've chosen. Your father, on the other hand, is dealing with the brisk passage of time, the end of an era, and the loss of his special daughter.

Understanding Your Father's Feelings

How does a father feel as he prepares to give his daughter away in marriage? Just like George Banks, your father may have mixed emotions. He may understand intellectually that you are mature enough to marry but wonder if any man alive is worthy of your love. Jay Kesler, the former head of Youth for Christ, USA, says, "Giving a daughter away in marriage is like handing a beautiful, expensive, Stradivarius violin over to a gorilla."[1]

If a father is emotionally close to his

daughter, he will struggle with intense feelings of loss. He understands he must hand over his unchallenged place of power and authority in his daughter's life. In *Father of the Bride* George tells Annie to wear a jacket as she and her fiancé prepare to go out for the evening. Annie ignores his advice. But when her fiancé suggests she put on a jacket, she replies agreeably, "Okay." George's face registers his awareness that he has been replaced—already—by another man.

John Yates, senior minister at the Falls Church in Northern Virginia, reminisces about his daughter Allison's marriage to Will. "Intellectually I was happy with her decision. I kept trying to tell myself how wonderful it was, that this boy was an answer to our prayers, that Will couldn't have a better family, values, and habits. But deep down I had an impending sense of loss. I knew my relationship with my daughter was going to change and would never be the same again. I felt I was losing whatever control I had in her life."

What was most helpful to John during the months before the wedding? He says his talks with his daughter Allison helped ease his sadness—and there were several. "She was so sweet and affectionate. She kept saying she knew how hard it was for me and how much she loved me. In fact, she said she'd never love anybody like she loved me. Now I didn't want to usurp my future son-in-law's place, but I didn't want to lose that unique tenderness and affection either."

In spite of their bittersweet feelings, most fathers also feel great satisfaction when they look at their daughters and see all they have become. As they understand that their daughters are ready to become wives, they sense they have contributed significantly to their daughters' self-esteem, competence, and perceptions of themselves as women.

Tom, another father of the bride, admits, "At first I felt lighter. I realized I was shifting the responsibility for my daughter's well-being to another man. Soon I would no longer have to worry about her safety as she came home alone at night. Nor would I feel so personally concerned about her career decisions. Some other man would monitor the balance between her energy level and her personal ambitions." Knowing a daughter has chosen wisely engenders a profound sense of relief in the male heart and helps a father let her go. "Never underestimate the satisfaction a father feels if his daughter has chosen a decent, responsible man rather than a jerk," says Robert, a man who had given the "thumbs down" to his daughter's previous boyfriends.

And on the wedding day itself? All those tender feelings swirl together. Steve Brown, a minister and contributor to Bill McCartney's book *What Makes a Man?* saw both of his daughters marry within three months. He writes of his experience:

To be perfectly honest with you, I would have been far more sympathetic to fathers (and mothers) of brides over the twenty-eight years I was a pastor if I had only known what they were going through. They always seemed to be so happy and together. Now, having gone through it myself, I know they

were happy, but it was a bittersweet sort of happiness.... Did I cry? Are you crazy? Of course I cried. I didn't "blubber," but this crusty, old preacher did cry. I cried because of the memories. I cried because the ceremonies were so filled with meaning. I cried because God had been so faithful. I cried because I knew that, after this day, nothing would ever be the same.[2]

What If Your Relationship Isn't Close?

But what if your dad never connected emotionally with you in the first place? What if your father and mother divorced and he never saw you grow up? Before her March wedding, one father sent his daughter a Valentine with a picture of a little girl on the front, a child about the age his daughter had been when he left home. This dad was grieving what never was, and never would be. He had not been around to watch his daughter grow up, and now she was getting married and saying good-bye to childhood forever.

In these instances a father may feel a keen sense of regret about a relationship that was never nurtured. If he has grown more reflective and sensitive over the years, he will likely feel sad because of missed opportunities. But it may be difficult for him to face his feelings, to acknowledge that he doesn't have warm, comforting memories of special moments with his daughter. He could even feel like a failure as a parent. Paul, who spent several years of his daughter's early life at sea with the navy, confides, "I looked back over the years and saw that though we did things together, my daughter and I were never really close. I was gone too often and for too long when she was a little girl. At some level I feel I have failed her as a father."

So what can a distant father do? If he can confront his feelings honestly and share them with a confidant or counselor, and ultimately with you, his daughter, he can set the stage for a more open, honest relationship in the present. We never outgrow our need for a positive relationship with our fathers. And sometimes we can forge adult bonds that bring healing to the past.

The Daughter's Response

But fathers aren't the only ones with strong feelings. Daughters are often surprised by the intensity of their feelings toward their fathers as they plan their weddings. As a daughter thinks about who will walk her down the aisle, she reflects on her relationship with her dad. If they have a warm, affectionate relationship, there is no question who will be by her side. Her father, of course. After all, he was the first man she ever loved, and he has been there during those important moments in her life. Through his love she has developed a sense of personal power that has made her more confident with men—employers, brothers, boyfriends, and now her fiancé.

The daughter who knows her father loves

her deeply is moved when she thinks of her dad "giving her away." How tender and evocative those words. They imply that someone who has been cherished, protected, and adored is about to be given up to another who will also cherish, protect, and adore. Having her father walk her down the aisle and give her to another man symbolizes a lifetime of love and care.

Even the daughter who has a distant or somewhat detached relationship with her father will probably not think twice about who will walk her down the aisle. But what is a given for her is a dilemma for the child of divorce. The woman whose parents divorced may feel keenly that, at this time of joy and anticipation, something vital is missing. Angela, whose parents divorced when she was five, says, "As I planned my wedding, I found myself thinking more about my biological father than I had in years. It wasn't that I didn't love my stepfather; he basically raised me. But I felt so, so sad that my real father had been uninvolved in my life. Because he left, I felt he had forfeited any right to walk me

down the aisle and give me away. Really, he gave me away years before."

Most brides want the person closest to them to walk them down the aisle, whether this is a biological father, stepfather, uncle, grandfather, or even mother. An older couple may choose to walk down the aisle together, showing by their action that they are independent of their parental homes. Sara, a social worker, chose her mother to escort her to the altar. After all, her dad had left when she was very young, and her mother had gone to work to support herself and her daughter. "My mom was the one I wanted to honor," says Sara firmly.

When I thought about telling my father that I wanted my stepfather to give me away, I grew anxious. My stepfather raised me, but I didn't want to hurt my daddy's feelings. Although it would have been much easier to tell Daddy over the phone, I felt it was important to talk to him in person. I wanted to be kind, to affirm his role in my life. I told him that while I had asked my stepfather to walk me down the aisle, Greg and I really wanted him to be a part of the wedding ceremony. Would he do a reading? He sat silently for a few minutes, then said quietly that he would 'be honored' to participate. I was so relieved. As it turned out, he was not only generous financially, but he and my stepmother never made me pay a price for my decision. I will be forever grateful that they cared more about my feelings than about any particular role in my wedding.

KRISTEN

While some divorced fathers take the high road, others do not. They react to their daughters' decision with great bitterness and anger. Janice remembers the impact her painful decision and her father's reaction had on their relationship.

My parents divorced when I was thirteen, and both eventually remarried. Over the years I developed a good relationship with my step-father, but he wasn't really a father figure. So the decision of who would walk me down the aisle was difficult. I thought about my brother or mother, but I decided to walk by myself, thinking that way nobody would get hurt.

But my father had assumed he would give me away. When I told him about my decision, he screamed at me over the phone, 'How could you do this?' and we ended up having a huge fight. All my feelings about him and his lifestyle that had been stored up for years spilled out.

When my fiancé, Ralph, and I sent out invitations, Dad responded that he and my stepmother would not be coming to our wedding. Part of me was glad—there would be less tension. But Ralph was surprised. He was from an intact family and didn't understand my splintered family. Ralph even called my dad the day before our wedding and begged him to come, but Dad refused. On my wedding day I was relieved he wasn't there. However, we didn't speak for three years after that.

Janice's situation was heart wrenching. It's tragic when parents choose to work their own agenda at the bride and groom's expense. If you want to have someone other than your father walk you down the aisle and your father refuses to accept your decision gracefully, hear him out. But maintain your integrity. You have the right to ask the person closest to you to give you away. The choice is ultimately yours.

You May Improve Your Relationship with Your Dad

On a positive note, the months before a wedding can be a time to begin work on a difficult or painful father-daughter relationship. Sometimes a daughter needs to take the initiative and examine her heart. Jessica's dad had been a workaholic when she was growing up, but Jessica felt she needed to ask her father for forgiveness for shutting him out of her heart and her life. So she called and asked if they could have lunch together. She began their conversation by saying she had been thinking about their relationship and wanted to improve it. "I know you made overtures to me when I was a teenager, but I pushed you away. Will you forgive me? I want to have a clean slate when I walk down the aisle, and I realize my relationship with you will affect my relationship with Jim." Jessica's father was touched and responded by asking her to forgive him for not being there when she was a little girl, for being too caught up in other things. "I felt so much freer when I left the restaurant that day," says Jessica. "What a relief, and how much better I felt on my wedding day."

Whatever your relationship with your father, understand that your wedding will be an intense, emotional moment for both of you. If you are fortunate enough to have a close bond with your father, your wedding day will add to the rich store of memories you have from childhood. And if you and your father have a distant or painful relationship, you can use this time to begin to make peace with each other. When both of you are open to finding new, common ground, some honest conversations could initiate a warmer, more open adult relationship.

After the Wedding

But how will your dad feel once the wedding guests have departed and only the rice, presents, and wilting flowers remain? Perhaps better than you would expect. He may view this time as an opportunity to receive more of your mother's attention. For years your parents' energies have been focused on raising and launching you and your siblings. A wedding day officially and symbolically marks the end of child rearing for you. All of that nurture can now be poured back into your parents' marriage. Even if you have lived on your own for years, your parents will sleep better, knowing you have someone who loves and cares for you.

In *What Makes a Man?* author Steve Brown affirms that he and his wife, Anna, are enjoying life after children:

Anna and I are starting a new life too… establishing new memories and new ways of doing things. We…are looking forward to what God has planned for the future. We are getting reacquainted, traveling together and feeling free of the constant responsibility that parents feel for their children.… The house seems bigger than it did, and it is a lot quieter. There are empty places that were filled with the laughter of our daughters. Sometimes there is loneliness. The empty nest and vacant bedrooms are filled with memories. Isn't that bad? No, that's good. How do we like it? I'm glad you asked. We like it a whole lot![3]

Some parents even find romance rekindled as they spend time around the newlyweds. "Being around all that adoration and submerged passion definitely has had a positive effect on my marriage," laughs Jeff, whose fourth and last child recently married. "The empty nest? I've waited for it for years."

Chapter Five

THE INVISIBLE ONES:
THE PARENTS OF THE GROOM

Do not press me to leave you or to turn back from following you!

Where you go, I will go; Where you lodge, I will lodge;

your people shall be my people, and your God my God.

RUTH TO HER MOTHER-IN-LAW, NAOMI

RUTH 1:16

Erma Bombeck knows what it's like to be the groom's mother. America's suburban humorist says of her son's marriage: "It was the first thing he had ever done in his entire life to make me happy."[1] On her son's wedding day Erma wore beige and kept her mouth shut. She understood the traditional role of the groom's mother: stay invisible. But her son and his new wife understood a deeper truth—that all the love and commitment she had given to her son and his new marriage needed to be recognized and applauded.

On the night of the wedding just as Erma and her husband of forty-four years had turned off the light in their hotel room, the phone rang. It was their son and his new wife, calling because they hadn't had a chance to say good-bye. Although Erma wisecracked, "Get a life!" she was deeply touched. As she lay in the darkness musing about marriage—her own and her son's—she felt blessed, knowing that her son and his bride would soon learn what she and her husband already knew: that each new day brings its own joys and challenges.[2]

Bombeck must have felt honored that she and her husband were so significant to the newlyweds. Unfortunately many parents of the groom feel invisible and fear that their tastes and wishes may not be considered in planning the wedding. They play a supporting role compared to the central roles of the parents of the bride. Granted, they host the rehearsal dinner and may even contribute to wedding costs and possibly a honeymoon. While some parents are relieved to have a minor role in the planning process, others, particularly the groom's mother, may chafe at being left out.

Since your fiancé's parents will be key players for the rest of your lives, it's important to understand their feelings and to honor their new role in your life.

Introducing the Mother of the Groom

Within your groom's family the central player is your future mother-in-law. Let's face it. Since we women are the intimacy experts in our families, the men are usually more than willing for us to schedule all those family get-togethers and to gather the family news. So who is this other woman you will soon be connected to by marriage, telephone lines, and family holidays? Although the culture has stereotyped a mother-in-law as a cross between a bloodhound and a vulture, in truth she is another mother—a possible surrogate mother, friend, and role model. Although she may not express them, she certainly has her own feelings about turning her son over to another woman. Some women do this with aplomb and grace; others have no little apprehension.

One mother-in-law who approached us at a conference said ruefully, "You raise your son all of his life for another woman, and you hope and pray that this woman does not spend the rest of her life criticizing his mother." This mother-in-law had no daughters and had somewhat distant and painful relationships with the wives of her three sons. She says of her daughters-in-law, "One can't stand her own mother, and the others are too new on the scene to know well yet."

Relinquishing the Role of Number One Woman

As you begin to know this woman who raised your fiancé, try to see your upcoming marriage through her eyes. Most mothers of the groom feel some loss when their sons marry. They are aware of the truth in the old adage, "Your son's your son till he gets him a wife; your daughter's your daughter all of her life." Psychological research shows that while daughters typically remain close to their mothers throughout their lives—calling them frequently or even moving to the same town once the children are born—this is less common with sons.

Since women traditionally nurture family relationships through calls, notes, and visits, your new mother-in-law may wonder if she will still be able to call her son and have open conversations with him once he marries. And

59

will she ever see him alone again? There's reason for her concern. "Women are the ones who maintain family connections, defining family as their parents and siblings as well as their husband and children," says Matti K. Gershenfeld, a marriage and family therapist.[3] "Men see their family of origin as part of their lives, but when they marry, they transfer that sense of family to their wife and children."

No wonder some mothers greet the news of a son's impending marriage with mixed feelings. Linda Weber, author of *Mom, You're Incredible* and the mother of three sons, says that when her middle son, Blake, announced he planned to marry Jami Lyn, she felt conflicting emotions. While she was "happy he had found a woman who met his expectations," she knew it was the "end of the nurturing window." Linda explains, "For the mother of the groom this means a mom is no longer the number one lady in her son's life." Linda understood that letting go was the healthy thing to do, but she was honest in admitting it wasn't easy.

In working through her feelings, Linda wrote a poem for Jami Lyn which talked about transferring the mantle of "number one" woman to her future daughter-in-law. To illustrate this rite of passage, Linda not only read the poem aloud at the rehearsal dinner but gave Jami Lyn a unique gift: two severed apron strings. For Linda, giving the poem and the apron strings signaled her willingness to let go of her son and to welcome Jami Lyn into the family.

Losing the role of "number one lady" naturally generates ambivalent feelings, and this probably has little to do with you personally. Your future mother-in-law may think you're wonderful yet still worry about her ability to stay close to her son and to have an ongoing and meaningful role in his life. Will she ever have those heart-to-heart talks with him again, or will you always answer the phone?

One woman who loved and accepted her daughter-in-law still struggled with the fact that she never saw her son alone. He was married for eight years before he came home alone for a weekend, and even then it was because he was in town on a business trip. "We love our daughter-in-law," says Mary Alice, "but it was wonderful to be the original family for just a few days." Gladys, a southerner and wise, older woman, told a young bride, "Encourage your husband to spend some time alone with his parents. They'll love you for it. This doesn't mean they don't care about you. It just means they need to have their boy back home occasionally."

As you get to know your fiancé's mother, keep in mind that both you and she are entering a new territory called the Land of In-laws. At this point you don't know what to expect, but neither does she. Right now you have little shared history. "We do not share a history— the long, loving history that I have with my boys and that Liz shares with her parents," states Claire Berman of her relationship with her new daughter-in-law. "As a result, we don't take each other for granted, as family members do. A daughter? Ours is not yet the kind of parent-child relationship that makes it safe to say almost anything—thoughtful or thoughtless—

to one another and forget it the next minute."[4]

The fact that you lack this shared history simply means you have a future to look forward to. Together you can plan holidays, family vacations, shopping excursions. If children come, you both can love them wholeheartedly, and this will create a common bond. If you and she are open to friendship, and if you're both willing to accept each other, you may discover you have another mother.

"She has accepted me thoroughly," Linda Weber says of Jami Lyn. "She calls me 'Mom' and has written me precious letters. She has also captured my vision of the importance of nurturing children." What has helped their relationship? Linda was sensitive enough to understand that, between women, control can be a big issue. "Because I was able to give Blake to Jami Lyn, she has loved me all the more."

The first Christmas after her marriage, Jami Lyn followed Linda's example by writing a poem about their new friendship and decorating it with flowers from the rehearsal dinner which she had carefully dried. The poem begins:

You are the other mother that I received the day I wed your son. And I just want to say thank you, Mom, for the loving things you've done. You've made me feel extra special as first daughter among the ranks. You've given me a gracious man with whom I share my life.

When a mother-in-law genuinely relinquishes her son, chances are she will be rewarded. "Jami Lyn has given back to me love from both of them," Linda remarks.

Acceptance Works Both Ways

Of course, some brides are more open to having another mother than others are. What makes the difference? If you have a close relationship with your own mother, you are more likely to welcome another mothering figure into your life and trust her. On the other hand, if you have had a painful or emotionally distant relationship with your mother, you

may transfer some of these feelings to your future mother-in-law. Since our mothers teach us our first lessons about love, intimacy, and women—starting in infancy—it's not surprising that these attitudes and expectations affect our relationships with other women, including our prospective mother-in-law.

But even if you have had a rocky relationship with your mother, you now have a second chance to receive mothering. The relationship a woman has with a mother-in-law is usually less intense, less complicated than the one she has with her own mother. For this reason she only stands to gain if she can forge a warm bond with her future husband's mother.

Karen, who has been married for four years and is now pregnant with her first child, talks about her newfound family and mother-in-law, Eleanor: "When I married Peter, I inherited a huge family. I've had rough times in my own family, but Peter's family provides a lot of stability. My mom was busy with her own life when I planned my wedding—she didn't want to be involved or to interfere. But

I wanted someone to interfere! So Ellie became what I wish my own mother had been. She helped me with the shopping and wedding music. Together we found a caterer. Ellie treated me like a daughter and made me feel as if I were already a part of her family. What's more, she's given me unconditional acceptance." Karen continues, "I feel I have two moms now: twice the love, twice the attention."

And for those who have close, secure ties with their mothers? Then a mother-in-law need not supplant this original mother-daughter bond. In this case, the mother-in-law can become a treasured friend. When Pam married Andy, her mother-in-law, Phyllis, asked her to call her "Mom."[5] Pam, who was close to her own mother, couldn't imagine doing this, but she was quick to reassure her mother-in-law she loved her just the same. Over the next fifteen years the two women became ardent pen pals and visited frequently. Pam's children loved Phyllis and said of her, "Grandma gives the softest hugs."

Although the two women didn't have a lot in common, both were committed to home and family life and both loved the color purple, or so Pam thought. Across the years, until Phyllis died in 1990, they exchanged gifts, frequently something lavender or purple. Only in discussing funeral arrangements with Phyllis's sister did Pam learn that pink, and not purple, was her mother-in-law's favorite color. Touched by Phyllis's efforts to have something in common—even just a favorite color—Pam laid a lavender iris in Phyllis' casket. After all, for fifteen years they had shared the color purple.

63

Creating Ties that Bind

So how can you get your relationship with your fiancé's mother off to the best start and begin to create warm ties? Soon after you become engaged, involve her in the wedding plans. Why not ask her to have lunch with you and talk to her about your ideas? Find out what her expectations are, what recommendations she has for florists, caterers, reception sites. If your future mother-in-law is included in the planning, she will probably have fewer feelings of loss and will make an easier transition into the role of mother-in-law.

Introducing the Father of the Groom

Although you will spend more time with your future mother-in-law at showers and luncheons, don't forget your fiancé's dad. What does the father of the groom experience once an engagement is announced? One of his chief concerns is whether or not his son has chosen a good woman. Are you a good match for his son intellectually, emotionally? Do you have worthy values? What about your strength of character, your virtues? Will you be a good mother? Carve out some time with your future father-in-law so he can get to know you and understand that his son has made a wise choice. Then he will be more supportive of your marriage.

Although they may not articulate their feelings to anyone but their wives, fathers also experience a sense of loss when their sons marry. When asked if he talked to his twenty-three-year-old son about his feelings, one father simply said, "There wasn't time." But years later he still feels a keen loss and sadness.

Some fathers are a bit anxious about how the new woman will fit into their family. Elliott admitted to some uncertainty when his son Mark married Su. "You've raised your son and so he's a known quantity," states Elliott. "But you don't know this new woman, and that makes things unpredictable." He is quick to add, however, that he thinks Su is a great match for Mark.

Although some fathers of the groom are concerned about how marriage will change their relationship with their sons, many happily discover they spend more time with their sons after marriage than before. A marriage often ushers in an opportunity for a father to get to know his son as an adult—man-to-man. And as their women invest time in their new relationship, men may have time for golf, fishing, tennis, or lunch. Eric and his father shared a weekly lunch date during the first months following the wedding. Since they had been too busy for this prior to the wedding, they felt fortunate to have time together, more time alone than they had experienced for years.

The Rehearsal Dinner

Although the groom's parents traditionally have a relatively minor role in the wedding itself, they do host the rehearsal dinner. This event can be an intimate gathering filled with meaning as friends, family, and members of the wedding party spend several hours together the night before the wedding. Here the father of the groom is in the spotlight. He sets the tone of the evening with his opening remarks.

In addition to hosting the rehearsal dinner and making it a warm, personal affair, the father of the groom, along with the father of the bride, has the opportunity to offer a toast or confer a blessing on his son and new wife.

When Greg married Sunnie, Greg's father, Jerry Regier, founder of The Family Research Council, chose to bless his son at the reception.

Why confer a personal and marital blessing? In keeping with the Old Testament patriarchs who verbally blessed their children, Jerry says, "To bless someone is to 'bow the knee,' to give high honor and high value to the person blessed. We bless others, not because of what they've done for us, but because of who they are."

Although many Jewish families continue to confer blessings on their children, this is not a usual practice for Christians. Nonetheless, Jerry and Jim, Sunnie's father, carefully crafted their words, and each blessed his own child, placing both hands on his child's head in much the same style as the ancient patriarchs. The following is an excerpt of Jerry and Sharyn's blessing given to Greg.

Greg, your mother and I have thoroughly enjoyed seeing you grow up. When you came into our home in October 1970, twenty-three years ago, the excitement level went up several decibels.

Greg, you are our firstborn son, and you have always been our energetic live wire, loving every minute of life and not ever wanting to miss out on anything. As your mother said last night, you always wanted to be around other people because you value friendship more than things, and relationships more than possessions.

You have blessed our lives with your creative and boundless energy, your love for your friends, and your positive, can-do attitude toward life. You believe that it is okay to dream and that dreams can become a reality...that everything is possible. And it is.

Your mother and I have learned from you the value of fun, of honesty, and of friendship.

Greg, you are like walking into a dark room and turning on the light. You brighten up everything around you. You are also like running through a sprinkler on a hot day...or like turning on the radio and hearing your favorite song. You have that kind of effect on those around you.

But Greg, you are also like an anchor on a ship because you are secure in who you are, and you know what your heritage is...and you are proud of it.

Greg, Sharyn and I bless you today and pray that God will take your creative energies, your friendly personality, and your love of life and fun and will infuse that into your marriage...and that God will use those characteristics in your future law studies and career for His honor and the enrichment and encouragement of others.

We admire you and love you very much and wish you all of God's goodness with Sunnie.

And so it goes from one generation to the next. Families intertwine with families, creating a rich tapestry. As your parents confer their blessings on you and your fiancé at this special time, so one day you may pass along a part of their heritage to your children. What better time than now to begin weaving these life-enhancing relationships?

Chapter 6

AMONG SISTERS AND FRIENDS

Few comforts are more alluring for a woman than the rich

intimate territory of women's talk.... A woman friend will say,

"You are not alone. I have felt that way, too.

This is what happened to me." Home, in other words.

ELSA WALSH, REPORTER FOR THE WASHINGTON POST

The last-minute question asked of every bride is not, "Are you sure you want to go through with this?" but rather, "Do you have to go to the bathroom?"

Having answered yes, the bride and her matron of honor sister scrambled upstairs and into the ladies' room of the Chicago church. Upon finishing, the bride leaned over to pull up her assorted lingerie. But while she had somehow been able to push everything down, she found she couldn't pull anything back up. The boning in both her backless, strapless bra and her...strapless wedding dress rendered her immobile. "It was like trying to bend your ankle in a ski boot," she recalls.

It was a humiliating moment for the thirty-three-year-old independent career woman—and it would have been a terrifying one, as well, if she had been alone. But she wasn't. The bride waddled out of her stall and plaintively asked Big Sister to be of assistance. "Well, I taught you how to walk," said the sister, struggling to return the bride's panties, pantyhose, and girdle to their rightful position.

"The least I can do is pull up your pants on your wedding day!"[1]

As participants in your upcoming wedding, your friends and sisters will play a central role in ensuring its success, providing help that ranges from the sublime to the hilariously mundane. But even more than their physical help, you will need their emotional support and sense of humor.

The Support of Soul Mates

Women need other women, cradle to grave, and they especially need them during the stressful moments of life. So important are our female friends that we describe them as "encouragers," "supporters," "soul mates," "confidantes." With our sisters and friends we unburden our hearts. We've learned since our first friendships as four-year-olds to nurture each other when our spirits flag, to stand by each other when life is good or comes crashing down around our feet. So it's natural with our shared histories and intertwined lives that our sisters and friends are closely involved in our wedding—one of the biggest events of our lives.

In *The Sister Bond* Toni A. H. McNaron writes, "A sister can be seen as someone who is both ourselves and very much not ourselves—a special kind of double."[2] More than any peer, your sister understands why you are the way you are—she shares your family background and life experiences. "I love my sister very much," says Alison, recently married. "And who better to be with me at life's biggest moment? After all, she was the one who snuck me Flintstone's vitamins, carried my diaper bag, and made me nachos and pizza when I was a struggling college student."

And if they're married, our sisters can serve as pathfinders or trailblazers. A married sister has already dealt with those family relationships you will soon encounter. Who better understands how to deal with Mom and Dad or even crotchety Aunt Mildred? After all, she

has been over the wedding terrain already. With her advice and practical help, you can avoid some family minefields. She can also fill you in on the intricacies of married life.

Friends, too, occupy a special place in any wedding planning. When Catherine got engaged, Joanne spent numerous Saturdays with her best friend, poring over wedding books, looking at wedding gowns, selecting bridesmaids' dresses. Several weeks before her wedding, when Catherine injured her eye and failed a vision exam for her driver's license, she really needed Joanne's help. While Catherine underwent tests at the doctor's office, Joanne zipped around town, running last-minute errands and picking up wedding supplies. Happy to help, Joanne simply said, "My time will come."

Cindy says of her closest friend and bridesmaid, "Jeannette was a tremendous support. She shopped with me, encouraged me when I felt ragged, and painstakingly addressed scores of invitations and envelopes." The morning of Michelle's wedding day her friend Mary Beth

69

picked up her wedding dress for her at a nearby boutique. And when the women discovered that the plumbing had been cut off all over their apartment complex, they traipsed over to Mary Beth's parents' house to shower and prepare for the ceremony that afternoon.

Friends and sisters may also lend a sense of humor to diffuse a tense situation. Lori recalls her sister Susan's role. "My biggest fear was talking in front of all the people who attended our wedding—about 250. I thought I would get nervous and stutter during my wedding vows or throw up during the service. When I told my sister—at five o'clock in the morning the day of my wedding—she jokingly assured me she would put a bucket in the first row just in case."

What bride doesn't need the nurture these special women provide? Ann, a thirty-eight-year-old bride who married in December, recalls the help her friends and sisters provided on her wedding day. One friend came over at six o'clock the morning of her wedding to pray with her. And at eight, when Ann and her

bridesmaids arrived in a gaggle at a salon to have their hair styled, her sister walked in with a large basket brimming with pastries, juices, and coffee. "That set the tone for the day—a day when I felt loved and supported," says Ann.

When Your Friend Is Jealous

Although most brides feel supported by their friends during their engagement, jealousy may rear its ugly head. Remember, a wedding signals a change in the landscape of friendship. A new, and major, player has entered the scene. "Loyalties shift," says Karen, a thirty-five-year-old engineer. "While this is necessary, close friends do feel a sense of loss. Mine certainly did." The women in our lives have to accommodate a new person who occupies most of our thoughts and free time. While some friends or sisters graciously accept this change, others struggle.

Friendships with built-in flexibility and common values can survive the many transitions and stages of life—including marriage.

❦

Single friends, in particular, often have mixed feelings about the marriage of a valued confidante, and an older sister may suddenly become an insomniac when her younger sister marries first. How can they wholeheartedly celebrate that your search is over when theirs isn't? Feeling wounded by the cosmic unfairness of it all, these friends may be cool and distant at times during your engagement. Three years after the wedding one woman we interviewed is still hurt because of the way her best friend treated her. "She was obviously jealous and made me pay. I almost asked her not to be in the wedding party."

We found that women who marry in their early twenties tend to experience fewer problems with jealous or envious single friends. At younger ages friends aren't as worried about getting married themselves. On the other hand, brides in their late twenties and early thirties usually encounter some jealousy from at least one friend or sister.

Kelly, who is thirty, says her most difficult relationship during her engagement was with her maid of honor. "Robin and I had been very close friends," she says. "In fact, she was instrumental in my conversion to Christianity. As a result, I asked her to be my maid of honor even though I have a sister. But my engagement was really tough for her. Although she'd been in other weddings, this one hit her differently. I tried to keep the lines of communication open and understand her feelings, but it was hard at times. When Robin got a job offer in a different city, our relationship improved. That way, we each went on to something new and exciting."

But whether you marry in your early twenties or late thirties, your sister may be the one to feel the greatest loss. And that feeling is heightened when a sister moves away. Leanne, whose sister Beth married when she was twenty-three, said she wasn't concerned about marriage herself. She was sad that her sister—who had long been a confidante and trusted friend—was moving across the country. Now, three years later, Leanne is excited about the birth of Beth's first child. Though she is glad her sister is happily married, she admits ruefully the change wasn't easy for her.

Keeping Friends in the Landscape of Your Life

What can be done to prevent problems and strengthen important friendships during this transition time? In his book *Friendship: How to Give It, How to Get It,* Dr. Joel Block writes, "The friends most apt to last are those with whom we have shared crucial times and who change as we change; marital status is critical only if values and 'styles' become too discordant."[3] In other words, friendships with built-in flexibility and common values can survive the many transitions and stages of life—including marriage. We need our female friends at each stage of life, so use this critical time to strengthen your friendships by working through feelings and any tension.

SET ASIDE TIME FOR FRIENDS

To make the most of time with your friends, concentrate on the friendship itself. Jenise, a thirty-year-old who has been in a number of weddings, suggests, "The weddings that have been the most personal to me have been the weddings of three very good friends. These brides set aside time to spend with me, through weekends away or other special occasions." One recent bride says that pre-wedding time offers important opportunities to be gracious,

Bask in your friendships. See your friends as treasures,

not just people who need marching orders.

❧

to thank close friends, and to let them know how valued they are. She adds, "Bask in your friendships. See your friends as treasures, not just people who need marching orders."

Make sure you remember events in your friends' lives—birthdays, promotions, holidays. Celebrate with them, without always talking about your wedding. Listen empathetically to their struggles with husbands, boyfriends, jobs, families. While it's easy to be self-centered during this time, it's better to love and listen to others.

SET REALISTIC EXPECTATIONS

Put yourself in your friends' place, and give them time to adjust mentally and emotionally to your upcoming marriage. It's unfair to expect them to be as overjoyed and excited about your wedding as you are. If you lower your expectations, you may be pleasantly surprised at their responses.

Nicole, a recent bride who lives in New England, talks about a miscommunication with her friend Lisa that caused both considerable pain. "Right after Steve and I became engaged, I called Lisa to ask her to be in my wedding. Lisa and I became fast friends in college, and though we lived on separate coasts after graduation, I still considered her a close friend. I had always wanted her to be in my wedding, and we had even talked about it before Steve and I got engaged. So I was surprised and hurt when I asked her to be a bridesmaid and she gave a feeble yes. After stewing about it for two weeks, I called her back and said I felt she didn't want to be in my wedding. I tried to be rational. I recognized it would be expensive and time-consuming to fly from San Francisco to Boston. After I finished my prepared speech, Lisa reiterated her concerns about the distance. At that point, I was wounded. We both agreed she wouldn't be in the wedding."

Months passed. Nicole moved ahead with her wedding plans, but every time she thought about Lisa, she felt a twinge. She told herself that physical distance had caused them to grow apart. Still, it hurt.

Two months before her wedding, she decided to write Lisa a long letter about her feelings. Lisa promptly wrote back, explaining that she felt perplexed and confused. She had always planned on being in Nicole's wedding, but she needed for Nicole to be fully aware of all this would entail. Since Lisa had just graduated from law school and was starting a new job, she felt it would have been extremely difficult to be a long-distance bridesmaid. Even so, she was willing to do it.

Nicole was baffled. She wondered if she had misread Lisa's initial response or if they had both misread each other. She decided to let it go. In the end the friends concluded they had misunderstood each other—and probably still did. But they affirmed their friendship. Nicole felt lighter. She was touched when Lisa flew to Boston from San Francisco for twenty-four hours, proof that Nicole's wedding meant a lot to her. As for Nicole, Lisa's presence meant the world.

BE SENSITIVE TO TIME DEMANDS

Time—or the lack of it—can become an especially sensitive issue. While nothing is as significant to you as your wedding, it's not necessarily at the top of your friends' lists. Although most bridesmaids enjoy shopping for dresses, addressing invitations, and helping you plan, they have other demands on their time—jobs and responsibilities, boyfriends or husbands, other friendships, and possibly children. It's important that you respect their commitments.

Also, you can help by prioritizing upcoming events. Tell your friends which parties, showers, or shopping trips mean the most to you and which are okay to miss. Understand that they can't make it to everything. Jane was troubled when her bridesmaid Sandra missed her shower. For days before and after she brooded over Sandra's absence, attributing it to lack of caring. When Jane finally told Sandra that she had hurt her feelings, Sandra was surprised. "I had no idea my presence meant so much to you," she said. Then she explained that she had recently broken up with her boyfriend and had felt unable to face a crowd of inquisitive women. As a result of their conversation, Jane was more understanding of her friend, and Sandra realized that her presence mattered.

In essence, planning a wedding can't be a one-way affair. Clarify your expectations early on, but try not to be disappointed when your friends have other demands on their lives. Both you and they need to be as sensitive and responsive as you can be.

Be Sensitive to Money Demands

Participating in modern weddings is seldom inexpensive as the following letter to Miss Manners shows.

Dear Miss Manners:

Now don't get me wrong. I am really a very proper person. So forgive me, Miss Manners, if my voice becomes shrill as I tell you this story.

My roommate was engaged to be married a year ago and asked me to be her bridesmaid. I tried my best, Miss Manners, really I did. For an entire year I chauffeured her around to photographers, addressed invitations, and planned menus. (Are salmon toasts suitable for a three o'clock reception, or is it more fashionable to have pink cottage cheese molded in the shape of a lamb?) I was forced to buy a hideous red bridesmaid's dress trimmed with cotton strawberries for eighty-five dollars. Red shoes to match for thirty-five dollars. And in July, I spent twenty-five dollars on a bridal shower after I found her copy of Emily Post tactfully left open to the page which stated that this was my social obligation. But I drew the line when she told me to buy four pink, plastic, midget carnations for my hair at eighteen dollars a pair. No, I said, and stood

75

my ground. No? She was incredulous. Hadn't I agreed to be her bridesmaid? Didn't I understand that it was her inalienable right to deplete my bank account of its entire contents, to render me poverty-stricken in the name of propriety? Tell me, Miss Manners, did I behave badly? I fear that I am unfit for polite society.

Gentle Reader:

Miss Manners congratulates you on your social fortitude. Miss Manners herself would have cracked before you did, at the pink cottage cheese, to be exact.[4]

You may laugh at this narcissistic bride and her beleaguered bridesmaid, and you may groan when you realize that your expenses today are much higher. But as you look for bridesmaids' dresses and accessories, remember that money may be a problem. Traditionally bridesmaids pay for their own dresses, shoes, lingerie, dress alterations, jewelry, and hair appointments. This can be pricey.

A bridesmaid can easily spend three to five hundred dollars by the time the wedding day rolls around. In addition, bridesmaids usually host showers for the bride and buy shower and wedding gifts. One bridesmaid spent five hundred dollars to be in a friend's wedding, which coincided with auto repairs and anxiety over a job layoff. For this bridesmaid, her friend's wedding preempted a vacation that year.

The bottom line? Select a dress your bridesmaids can afford. If necessary, look at lower-priced dresses from a catalog or discount store, or shop off the rack. You can also have attendants wear shoes or jewelry that most of them already own.

Advice from Bridesmaids for the Bride

To help you better understand your friends' needs, we interviewed a number of bridesmaids who told us what they appreciate from a bride-to-be.

❦ Don't wait too long to ask friends to be in your wedding. When you wait to ask, friends may become anxious or uncertain about their importance in your life. In addition, giving ample notice allows them to adjust their schedule and to allot money.

❦ Try to ask all of your bridesmaids within the same period of time. If your friends hear about others being asked, they may feel left out, or unwanted, or wonder why they were asked later.

❦ Reassure close friends that they're important. Many women worry they will be abandoned or replaced once a friend marries. Affirming friends enables them to relax and enjoy the wedding.

❦ Don't wait too long after the honeymoon to call. Friends will be eager to see you again and hear about your new life.

❦ Ask your friends about their lives. Don't be too self-absorbed. After all, if you enter into your friends' lives, they will feel more joyful for you. Brides who obsess about their weddings and their own lives strain their friendships.

❦ Plan some event—a luncheon, brunch, or breakfast—to celebrate with your bridesmaids. The event can also include other female wedding participants (your soloist, the readers) or female family members and can be held in a restaurant or a home. Either way, it's a nice idea for you to treat. If money is tight, prepare a casual luncheon yourself.

❦ Allow time for spontaneity in friendships. Although you have a hectic schedule, leave some unscheduled time before the wedding so friends don't feel like they have to pull out a calendar just to see you. Take the initiative. Ask a friend to meet you for lunch or coffee.

❦ At one of the pre-wedding celebrations (bridesmaids' luncheon, rehearsal dinner) tell guests how you met each bridesmaid and what her friendship means to you. Be sincere, even spontaneous, as you speak from your heart. Each of these women holds a special place in your life, and a pre-wedding gathering is a great place to affirm and honor them. Your friends will love it.

❦ Allow your bridesmaids to help with wedding tasks if they offer. But don't go overboard with your demands.

❦ Spend time alone with friends. If possible, plan an outing alone with each of your closest friends prior to your wedding—an afternoon tea, a shopping trip, lunches or dinners out, even working out together. If bridesmaids are in town, spend a night or weekend away with them. By laughing and reminiscing together, you may forget (momentarily) about wedding stresses and just enjoy your friendships. By the way, encourage your fiancé to have time with his buddies too. He needs to foster his same-sex friendships just as you do, and many grooms say they miss time with friends during the hectic days of the engagement.

❦ Don't be a micro-manager. Some brides like to control many details—color of stockings, the way bridesmaids wear their hair. While a uniform look is great, talk to your bridesmaids about their preferences as well.

❦ Thank your attendants and ushers with a gift. You needn't buy something expensive; however, a token of appreciation is customary and essential. Some possibilities include jewelry, address books, date books, frames, pictures, money clips, key chains. Many gifts can also be engraved with the attendants' names. If you have a flower girl, you should buy her a gift as well.

❦ Ask a bridesmaid to put together a "wedding first-aid kit" with emergency items such as aspirin, brush, bobby pins, makeup, glue, safety pins, hair spray, Saltine crackers, clear nail polish, Kleenex, needle and thread, breath mints, tape.

Brides Give Advice about Attendants

In addition to interviewing bridesmaids, we asked brides for tips on dealing with their attendants. They shared the following advice:

❦ Tell your friends and sisters how honored you are that they are in the wedding. You may choose to do this through notes, cards, toasts, gifts.

❦ If your fiancé has a sister, make a special effort to get to know her, even if she is not a bridesmaid. Consider giving her some responsibility in the wedding—as a greeter, candle lighter, or guest book attendant. This goes a long way toward creating good feelings within your new family, and you may find in time that she becomes a new friend.

❦ Add a bridesmaid rather than risk hurting someone's feelings. Most weddings don't have more than eight bridesmaids, but you have some leeway. If you aren't sure about the number you want, consider increasing the number of attendants rather than risk hurting a friend's feelings.

❦ Share the spotlight. Pre-wedding events are obviously for you, but drawing in other people won't diminish you or your place of honor. One bride purchased small gifts to give her bridesmaids at her shower and wrote notes telling each how important she was.

❦ Make time for each of your friends to get to know your fiancé. If your friends have an opportunity to begin a friendship with your fiancé, they will feel they are gaining a friend rather than losing one.

❦ Don't take all of your bridesmaids shopping with you for dresses. Trying to please everyone can push you toward a nervous breakdown!

❦ Don't ask bridesmaids what they would like as a gift. Chances are, none of them will want the same thing. Select a gift that is tasteful and affordable, and don't worry about finding the perfect gift for each individual. Otherwise, you will drive yourself crazy or spend yourself into the poorhouse.

❦ Set an early deadline for bridesmaids to submit money for dresses. If not, they may be late, and one girl can delay an entire shipment of dresses. Some brides have told us this caused them great anxiety. You need to manage those procrastinators!

❦ Finally, allow your friends to be themselves. Just as they must accept your foibles, you need to accept theirs. Try to provide opportunities for your closest friends to be honest about their feelings, and be ready to

79

work out any tensions. If you do, you'll keep your friends, and they will be grateful they shared your special day.

🌸 And don't forget your sisters. Although friends are key players in our lives, sometimes our sisters go the extra miles with us. Boon companions since birth, they are the veteran doll players and fellow girl scouts. These women have loved us, fought with us, and shared confidences across the years. So look for special times with a sister or, if you don't have one, a friend-sister.

During my engagement my sister Holly came through for me again and again. Not only did she go shopping for bridesmaids' dresses with two other bridesmaids, but she hung with me until I found the right one.

Initially I wanted input from all the bridesmaids, but each woman selected a different dress! (I soon realized that every woman has different body parts she wants to highlight or camouflage.) As a result we left the bridal shops that first day with absolutely nothing, and I was frustrated and anxious.

Several weeks later I decided to try again. Smarter this time, I only took my mom and Holly. As we hit the bridal shops early one Saturday morning, we asked Holly to model. A size six, Holly emerged from the fitting room time after time in dresses that were literally falling off her. (Many shops carry only larger-sized dresses for women to try on; individual sizes are ordered later.) Once Holly bounced out of the dressing room, clutching a voluminous red, size-sixteen jacket so she wouldn't expose herself to the bevy of shoppers, as the skirt trailed behind her. Mom and I burst into gales of laughter. I was touched that my sister was willing to spend her Saturdays gamely trying on dress after dress until we found the right one: a crimson dress that looked gorgeous on all my attendants on my wedding day.

What would we do without our sisters?

KRISTEN

Chapter Seven

THE MEANING OF MONEY

Superfluous wealth can buy superfluities only.

Money is not required to buy one necessary of the soul.

HENRY DAVID THOREAU

WALDEN

Friday, July 23, 1994. A gray and rainy morning dawns on the day Jackie is to have the wedding of her dreams in a romantic, wooded grove outside of Washington, D.C. For the occasion she wears an off-the-shoulder, Vera Wang gown—a dress with tiny sleeves and no train. "I didn't want it dragging in the mud," she says. She also decides against tulle and lace except for a veil she removes immediately following the ceremony.[1]

Jackie was the second daughter of Joan and Glade Flake to marry that summer, and both wanted large, formal weddings. Jennifer, twenty-six, chose to have a church wedding only six weeks before her younger sister married. While 175 guests attended Jennifer's problem-free wedding, 140 brave souls endured Washington's notorious midsummer humidity and drizzle to celebrate Jackie's special day.

Who paid for these weddings? Their father, Glade Flake, an attorney. To fund a wedding and reception for both daughters, Flake spent between twenty-five and thirty-five thousand dollars on each occasion—an unaffordable sum for most American families. But even the Flakes tried to economize, opting not to have air conditioning in the tent which they rented for the sit-down dinner—an extra six thousand dollars. They had five huge fans instead.

As it turned out, Jackie and her groom were married on the lawn under gray skies and experienced only momentary showers as they raced for the tent. Then, as an omen of blessing, the sun burst forth and a double rainbow graced the sky. While the band played, off came the jackets and the bridesmaids' pantyhose. And the parents breathed a sigh of relief.

Another couple, Steve and Renee Johnson, had a wedding on a more modest budget, and those who attended remarked on the beauty and charm of their autumn celebration. Like Jackie Flake, Renee wanted a garden theme, but she chose to bring the garden into the church. Small trees provided a backdrop for the purple and yellow flowers that adorned the altar, candelabra, and pews. To economize on decorations, Steve and Renee had an afternoon

Two of the first issues every couple must resolve are what kind of wedding they want and how much money is available to spend on it.

wedding and coordinated colors and flowers with a couple who married that morning. Their reception was catered at a graceful, old mansion on the grounds of a school. Guests remembered the lovely spread of fruit spilling from a cornucopia and cheeses, roast beef, and raw vegetables covering the tables.

Choosing a different path, Pam and Andy Goresh opted for a no-frills, no-fuss wedding when they tied the knot. Married in her back-yard under her favorite willow tree, Pam wore a fifty-dollar wedding gown purchased at a small boutique. She decided against a veil and high heels and instead wore white ballet slip-pers. Having just graduated from college, this bride wanted a worry-free wedding and invited only ten guests, all of them family. How does

she remember her wedding day? "I was very happy and it was a beautiful day. The wedding went off without a hitch. No one was hassled, no one was harried. My parents were thrilled. They love Andy, and I knew I couldn't have married a better guy."

Finally, when Richard and Patricia Gardner remarried in their late thirties, they elected to hold their wedding ceremony in a friend's home. Typical of the second time around, they elected to avoid pomp and circumstance. With little money and five children between them, they spent what funds they had on an exotic island honeymoon rather than an elaborate wedding. So for their wedding day brunch they asked about thirty friends to bring coffeecakes. The groom and host cooked breakfast—quiche, omelets, and delicious casseroles—for all of the assembled guests. Their total cost: two hundred dollars.

Who Pays and How Much?

Two of the first issues every couple must resolve are what kind of wedding they want and how much money is available to spend on it. While the bride's parents have traditionally hosted the wedding and reception, many couples today piece together their funding from different sources. Sometimes all of the parents contribute to the wedding and honeymoon, especially if couples are in their early twenties. According to a study by David Michaelson and Associates, some 52 percent of couples have both the groom's and bride's parents contribute to wedding expenses. But 71 percent of all brides and grooms today also make a hefty contribution to their wedding expenses.[2] We found this particularly true of couples marrying in their thirties and forties.

Often these older matches not only have mortgages to pay for, but they have savings accounts as well. Tara, a thirty-two-year-old, says she and her fiancé decided to pay for their wedding themselves, not only because they could afford to, but because they wanted to keep control of their wedding and felt they could only do so if they funded it.

Said another bride, "He who pays the most, controls the most." Cindy found this to be true and struggled with feeling less autonomous because her parents contributed funds and then dictated how the money should be spent. "It was hard," said this twenty-three-year-old high school teacher. "But the reality is that autonomy comes with a price. We could have been independent if Paul and I had paid for the wedding ourselves. Since we didn't have a lot of money, we viewed this as a last rite of passage—the last time we would need to ask our parents for money. It worked out just fine and we had a great wedding."

Those who need and want parental help

should go to their parents early on to determine a budget together. Since it's human to measure love by tangibles such as money, this can be an anxious process, particularly for children of divorce who feel insecure in their parents' love.

Divorce and Money

All too often an estranged husband and wife continue their warfare around the issues of kids and money. Children of divorce may grow up feeling bitter and resentful if their father's financial support has been a battleground for years. If this has been the case—and we are quick to acknowledge that some 50 percent of divorced fathers are fiscally responsible—then at the time of the wedding, old wounds are reopened. Daughters may find it painful and difficult to ask their divorced fathers for financial help. And those who do ask, run the risk of disappointment. Says one bride, "My dad had previously offered and promised to pay ten thousand dollars for the wedding. Now two and a half years later he has only paid five thousand dollars, and my husband and I have paid the rest."

What about those who have grown up with mothers who never remarried? All too often these children of divorce are acutely aware of their mothers' financial struggles and may hesitate to ask for help because they fear burdening their moms further. One bride remarked, "Since I had watched my mom struggle to live on child support and her earnings as a secretary, when Jon and I decided to get married, at first I didn't want to ask either parent for help."

Children whose parents are divorced are more often emotionally insecure than those who grow up in stable, intact families. Having missed some of the day-to-day gestures and tokens of love, as adults they look for tangible signs of parental love. Thus, key celebrations become even more perilous as those daughters hope, pray, their parents will be loving and kind in these emotionally heightened moments.

Sticker Shock

If you choose to ask your parents for help in paying for the wedding—whether your parents are divorced or not—don't be surprised at their initial shock at the cost.

I remember the evening Kristen and Greg came over to talk to us about how much we could contribute to their wedding and reception. As we four munched chips and salsa, Kristen, a veteran reader of Bride's magazine, began to tell us what she hoped we would fund. As she tallied up the cost, I groaned inwardly. "A wedding costs as much as a small car or a down payment on a house!" I muttered.

"Mom, you have no idea what a wedding costs in this city," Kristen replied, exasperated. "This is not the small southern town where you first married thirty years ago." As she patiently explained to us what the wedding of their dreams would cost, we decided

pretty fast we couldn't afford a sit-down dinner. And so the negotiation began. As I listened to Kristen, I couldn't help but remember the church reception my first husband and I had with cake, peanuts, and punch—an affair that cost several hundred dollars.

"Wouldn't you like to get married at home?" I asked, hoping to steer Kristen to what I thought was more affordable. She informed me tactfully that, no, she didn't want to be married at home, and that, in reality, it would be quite expensive to rent a tent. Also, where would a hundred and sixty people go to the bathroom? Knowing that our one-hundred-year-old farmhouse has antiquated plumbing, I could see her point. As Kristen and Greg worked with us, her naive parents, we learned that their dream wedding would cost about as much as Kristen's four years at the University of Virginia.

I felt overwhelmed. I went to bed that night, struggling with parents-of-the-bride sticker shock, a feeling that only increased in the days ahead as I discovered just how lucrative the American wedding industry is.

BRENDA

Do Your Homework First

So what can you do to lessen your parents' shock and ease the tensions in that first budget discussion? First, do your homework so you have an accurate idea of what a wedding costs. Understand that costs vary regionally and that weddings in metropolitan areas are considerably more expensive than in small cities or towns.

Here are some estimated costs for a traditional wedding by region.[3]

New England	$19,162
Mid-Atlantic	$18,203
South Atlantic (Carolinas, Georgia, Florida)	$15,856
East South Central (Louisiana, Mississippi)	$12,777
West North Central	$14,371
West South Central	$14,052
Pacific Northwest	$18,683
Rocky Mountain Area	$14,850

In addition to knowing the overall price of weddings, as part of your homework, research the relative costs of receptions, since it is the greatest single expense. Options include: a buffet meal, a sit-down luncheon or dinner, a catered meal in a historic setting, a catered reception at home, hors d'oeuvres, or a church reception.

By researching the costs of all the options, you will not only help your parents through what may be unfamiliar territory, but you can begin to pare down your own choices and determine what is most important to you. Every bride has different priorities. For one, the dress is all important. For another, the reception is critical. For a third, abundant flowers are foremost. So determine what matters most to you, make a list, and set your budget accordingly.

87

Many of the most significant parts of the ceremony

are completely unrelated to money.

❦

Money and Your Parents

Since a bride's wedding reflects, to some extent, her parents' willingness and ability to give, creating a budget can be enormously stressful for parents. Once your parents understand that options exist and that some are considerably more expensive than others, it will be easier to talk about what you and your fiancé desire.

But don't be surprised if your parents feel—at least at first—that what was good enough for them is good enough for you. They may be caught in a generational time warp and need time and some updated information to enter the era of modern weddings. Of course, if your parents have already had a daughter or son marry, they may be pros, and your job will likely be easier.

Equity among siblings is also a factor in determining a budget. "We had a lot of arguments at first," said one woman whose daughter chose a military wedding. "It was only after my husband and I sat down to figure out how much we could afford to give each of our four daughters that the smoke cleared. Our daughter had a smaller wedding than she wanted, but we told her we still have to pay for her sisters, and fair is fair." When one groom decided to take his bride to Hawaii and approached his parents for financial help, they gave him just enough money for a trip to Florida's Disney World. That was where his older brother had gone on the honeymoon their parents had funded.

Although your parents probably want to be open handed and generous, they may need some time to realistically assess what they can do. One father of the bride fumed for days after the initial money talk. He was chagrined at the inordinate prices that service providers charged and even threatened to quit his job and become part of the wedding industry conglomerate so he, too, could charge "outrageous" prices. Only as he got used to the idea that weddings are costly was he able to focus on his daughter's feelings and wishes. Even then, he insisted she cut costs wherever possible.

It's not unusual for parents to feel great pressure to spend, spend, spend. "We didn't want to appear cheap," said one beleaguered mother of the bride. She had already married off two sons, so she wasn't naive about wedding costs. But when her daughter married, she told friends that during the last weeks before the wedding she wrote so many checks she felt money was gushing from her veins. As she explained, "Unless parents split the cost, or the bride and groom contribute funds, the bride's parents end up carrying a heavy financial burden."

Although you want to have the wedding of your dreams, what if your parents offer to give more than they can comfortably afford?

Taking thousands of dollars out of a hard-won savings account is a big sacrifice, especially if this money represents years of labor and your parents are facing retirement. The truth is, many couples only begin to save significantly once their kids finish college, about the time the wedding bells start to ring.

Don't allow your parents to give more than they feel they can afford. It's important that they don't feel obligated to spend themselves into the poorhouse or go into debt to fund a wedding and reception that will be over in a few hours. Robbie, a salesclerk, told us that three years after her wedding, she, her husband, and her parents are still paying for a sit-down dinner for 175 guests. No reception is that important.

One midwestern minister and his wife had lived on a limited salary for years and had little savings, but they wanted their bright, articulate daughter to have more than they had experienced when they were married by a justice of the peace. So after some scrimping, dipping into their limited savings account, and much

89

creativity, they gave their daughter the traditional wedding of her dreams. Parishioners lavishly decorated the church with in-season flowers, and one of the church's superb cooks made a rose-laden wedding cake and tantalizing hors d'oeuvres. Although this family diminished their savings account for their daughter's wedding, all were satisfied with the end result.

Be Creative

In reality, the less money you have, the more creative you become. Lori remembers all the fun she had planning an affordable wedding: "To save money we opted for an outdoor reception under a tent at an old house—part of our church's property. My brother played classical music on his stereo, and my mom brought extra hanging baskets of flowers she had made for the occasion. In addition, we purchased two large, lovely arrangements from the florist. We decorated a swing suspended from an old oak tree with balloons, and we had an inexpensive, catered reception—a light lunch instead of a sit-down dinner."

I still remember a wonderful wedding I attended many years ago in England. The girls and I lived near London at the time, and early one Saturday morning we traveled with friends to the L'Abri Fellowship, a Christian study center, in Hampstead to attend the wedding of a couple we barely knew.

As we sat on folding chairs that morning, listening to Bach and Cat Stevens's "Morning Has Broken" on the stereo, the bride appeared, wearing a flowing, crimson dress that swished as she walked. Her long, dark hair was pulled back, and on top of her head was a broad-brimmed hat trimmed with red satin ribbons. Her groom was decked out as colorfully as she. For his wedding day, he had donned black trousers and a vest of brilliant colors.

This couple had become Christians only months earlier after traveling in Europe together. As part of their newfound faith, they

❧

wanted to honor God in their relationship through marriage. On this particular day they stood together and listened as Ranald McCaulay, the minister, spoke to them about the realities of commitment, about love that is not based on transient feelings but on faith in a holy, loving God, and a solid commitment to marriage and each other. As I sat among the celebrants, I felt deeply moved. A casualty of an unwanted divorce and a hurting single parent, I desperately needed to have my faith in the institution of marriage renewed. And it was—through that simple, redemptive wedding ceremony.

After the wedding we adjourned to the large parlor of this old English manor house for a square dance. The wedding cake, baked by the bride the day before, was slathered with chocolate icing and M&Ms. It was, for years, the loveliest and happiest wedding I

attended. True, it wasn't traditional, but it was a union of two lives, heralding a new marriage and a new beginning.

BRENDA

What's essential is that your wedding is a meaningful, wonderful experience. The only people who will know what your wedding cost are you, your fiancé, and your parents. Wedding guests come simply to be part of this timeless, joyful experience. They come to be with you, to rejoice in your good fortune, hoping to be touched themselves. Said one couple, "Let your friends and family see what's important to you. Let them see your heart and understand something of your love for each other." Remember, many of the most significant parts of the ceremony are completely unrelated to money: the vows, toasts, loving rituals that you and your groom create, and the aura of the day.

91

Besides, it's possible to have all the pomp and glitter and leave guests feeling their presence wasn't important. Sally remembers a wedding on Long Island that took place in a large, imposing church with a reception at the local country club. She and several friends drove all night to attend this wedding of college friends. Unfortunately they arrived too late for the ceremony, and when they showed up a half-hour into the fabulous reception, they were stunned to discover few people remained. A small orchestra played to a virtually deserted room. The bride, groom, and all their parents had already exited, and these weary guests wandered aimlessly in a daze. Says Sally, "The food was great—there were masses of it—but it certainly wasn't worth all those hours in the car."

A Final Word

Every bride desires a beautiful and memorable wedding, but in the final analysis, this can't be bought. The fox in Antoine de St. Exupery's classic, *The Little Prince*, tells his friend that "what is essential is invisible to the eye." So it is at every wedding. While your guests will be duly impressed by the flowers, the beauty of the setting, the bridesmaids' dresses, your glorious gown, they will also be looking for something "invisible to the eye."

And some couples in the pews, as they hear you and your groom speak those ancient vows, will reach over and take their spouses' hands. They will renew their own marital vows in their hearts as they are reminded of the holiness of matrimony. One wife said that after she and her husband attended a moving, deeply spiritual wedding, he got in the car and sobbed as he drove down the freeway. "I have not loved you well," he confessed. A year later his wife says, "That wedding was a turning point in our marriage."

This holy, convicting, life-changing moment no amount of money can buy.

Chapter Eight

Love's Masterpiece: Your Wedding

When love and skill work together,

expect a masterpiece.

JOHN RUSKIN

What makes a wedding beautiful? An event that goes perfectly, smoothly, and according to plan? "No," says Suzanne, who has been married to David for eight years. "I have been to many simple weddings that were more beautiful than lavish ones.... If the couple is in love, and the wedding is an expression of their love, then beauty shines through." Angela, who has been a bridesmaid numerous times, adds: "It's what a couple reveals of themselves that makes a wedding meaningful." Charlene, a new wife, agrees, "Things do come together in the end, even if small details don't go according to plan."

To plan a successful wedding, you and your groom will need lots of heart and a bit of skill. A wedding provides the opportunity for you and your fiancé to create an event that represents your joint beliefs, priorities, favorite music, colors, flowers, and tastes. It's an event that honors your mutual love and enduring pledge to each other. While this chapter will help you with the "skill" part, making your wedding unique and personal is up to you.

What to Do

Over the next several weeks and months you will have dozens of decisions to make. Now is the time to get organized and to set a plan so you can enjoy your wedding day and all the festivities that lead up to it.

To help you get started, we suggest the following timeline, tasks, and priorities. Of course, your timetable may differ, depending on the length of your engagement and kind of wedding you are planning.

Your Wedding Calendar

SIX MONTHS TO ONE YEAR BEFORE

❦ Select the ceremony site.
❦ Decide on the kind of reception.
❦ Book the reception site.
❦ Choose and order the wedding dress.
❦ Decide on the wedding colors.
❦ Book the photographer.

❦ Book a videographer.

❦ Choose and order the bridesmaids' dresses.

❦ Reserve lodging for out-of-town guests.

❦ Book the florist and select floral arrangements.

❦ Choose the rehearsal dinner site.

❦ Begin planning the honeymoon.

❦ Meet with the minister.

❦ Plan the ceremony and music.

THREE TO FOUR MONTHS BEFORE

❦ Choose and order the invitations.

❦ Register for wedding gifts: china, linens, cookware.

❦ Book musicians or a deejay.

TWO TO THREE MONTHS BEFORE

❦ Select and order the wedding cake.

❦ Have your fiancé arrange for wedding attire for himself and the groomsmen.

ONE TO TWO MONTHS BEFORE

❦ Address and mail the invitations.

❦ Order your wedding rings.

❦ Select and print the wedding programs.

❦ Purchase or order the wedding favors.

❦ Begin fittings for your wedding dress.

ONE MONTH BEFORE

❦ Go with your fiancé to obtain a marriage license.

❦ Plan the seating for the reception.

❦ Write out place cards for the guests.

❦ Print directions to the reception and rehearsal dinner.

❦ Follow up with service providers.

95

Speaking Practically

Let's look at each task on your timeline.

THE CEREMONY SITE

About 80 percent of all wedding ceremonies are held in churches; however, homes, gardens, or the reception site are also possibilities. The time of day and the formality of the ceremony will greatly influence your decision. Some churches reserve a number of days each month just for members, and may reduce the cost for members as well.

Reception site possibilities are numerous: a restaurant, ballroom, hotel, home, women's club, country club, meeting hall, historic site or inn, private school, old mansion, garden or park, or your church's fellowship hall.

After selecting the location, you and your fiancé will need to decide if you want to serve a meal. You can choose from a sit-down lunch or dinner, an informal buffet, or a morning brunch, or you can have a reception with light hors d'oeuvres or simply cake, fruit, and finger food. Whichever you choose, be sure to sample all of the food ahead of time.

How formal do you want your wedding to be? Typically the formality of the reception is determined by the time of day (evening weddings are the most formal), the number of guests, the bride's wedding attire, and the kind of reception (sit-down meals are more formal than buffets). Once you and your fiancé decide about the formality of your wedding, you can choose decorations, flowers, and bridesmaids' dresses.

The reception is usually the single greatest wedding expense, so make sure you have an accurate per-person cost that fits within your budget. Ask questions about all costs involved. For example:

- Is there a cake-cutting fee?
- Are taxes and gratuities included in the per-person estimate? If not, ask for a revised estimate that includes them.
- Is there a caterer that the hotel/ballroom works with regularly? Does the hotel require patrons to use this caterer?
- Are decorations included in the price? Which decorations will be available on the proposed day?
- Are linens for the tables available? Is there an additional cost to use them?

Since the reception is so costly, it's a good place to begin trimming costs if necessary.

Here are some money-saving tips:

❦ Have a sit-down meal rather than a buffet.

❦ Have your wedding midafternoon and serve a light lunch, hors d'oeuvres, or cake rather than a dinner.

❦ Have the reception at home or at the church.

❦ Decrease the size of the guest list (an easy way to save).

❦ Have friends cater the reception.

❦ With the help of family and friends, prepare some of the food yourself ahead of time.

THE WEDDING DRESS

If you are planning to order a dress, shop early. Some bridal boutiques require up to five months to deliver a dress. If you are going to have a portrait taken, you will need even more time. Also allow plenty of time for alterations and emergencies. (One bride had to send her dress back to the factory two weeks before the wedding because of a defect in the material. Fortunately, after much hand wringing, she received her dress just in time.) As you calculate the cost of the dress, be sure to include an estimate for other expenses: a headpiece and veil, petticoat, shoes, jewelry, lingerie, alterations.

Some boutiques have rooms with dresses in particular price ranges so customers only try on those they can afford. Other stores sell dresses off the rack, thus dispensing with an ordering or a waiting period. And consignment stores sell dresses that have been worn once or twice. Ann, a recent bride, recommends buying a secondhand dress. "It amounts to a fraction of the cost, and the store will give you half of whatever they receive when they resell the dress." Or, consider borrowing a dress from a friend or relative.

Other tips for saving money on your wedding dress:

❦ Buy a dress that needs no alterations.

❦ Buy a dress from an outlet store.

❦ Buy a dress in a less expensive fabric.

WEDDING COLORS

Choose wedding colors early, since your selection will guide your choices of flowers, bridesmaids' dresses, and decorations. Be sure to think about seasonal changes in colors as well as the availability of flowers during certain times of the year. If the wedding is planned for the fall or winter, darker, richer colors and heavier fabrics are appropriate; if the wedding is in the spring or summer, both colors and fabrics can be lighter.

THE PHOTOGRAPHER

Pictures are the principal remembrance after your wedding day is long gone, so choose your photographer carefully. In fact, most of the brides we interviewed said a good photographer was the one item they were not willing to skimp on, even if they were on a tight budget. We recommend choosing a photographer who specializes in weddings rather than relying on just any professional photographer.

Since your wedding moments can never be recaptured, the photographer must understand your priorities ahead of time. Specify which shots are important to you—coming down the aisle, exchanging rings, getting into the car, starting the first dance, cutting the cake.

A note of caution here. Hiring a friend or relative as the photographer can lead to problems. One bride chose a photographer who was a friend of her future mother-in-law. So while the mother-in-law was a smiling presence in almost all of the shots, the photographer failed to capture many significant moments, such as the bride coming down the aisle, the first dance, and even cutting the cake. This distraught bride sobbed when she saw her proofs.

Finally, if you choose a freelance photographer, have a contingency plan. People do get sick and have accidents. For this reason, you and your family may feel more comfortable using a studio with several photographers who can pick up your assignment if your chosen photographer can't make it.

VIDEOGRAPHER

If you want a unique way to remember your wedding, have a videographer record it. If you and your fiancé decide to hire a videographer, ask how many cameras will be used, whether the video will be edited, and whether the videographer will be working solo or with a team. As with the other service providers, you would be wise to review his past work.

Some money-saving tips:
- ❦ Tape only the ceremony.
- ❦ Purchase an unedited version of the tape.
- ❦ Have a skilled friend videotape the wedding.

BRIDESMAIDS' DRESSES

Bridesmaids' dresses are usually in one of the wedding colors and should complement the bride's gown. Consider also the formality and time of your wedding. Choose a dress that you like but one that will be flattering to your attendants in color and style.

Boutiques should indicate whether the catalog or dress sample is appropriate for the season of year for your wedding. As you would expect, the dresses displayed in July are not the same ones displayed in December. Consult with the mother of your flower girl as well, so she can buy a dress for her daughter which complements the wedding gown or matches the color of the bridesmaids' dresses.

LODGING AND RESERVATIONS

Once you have chosen the location for the ceremony and reception, you can reserve lodging for out-of-town guests. Most hotels/motels offer group rates for blocks of rooms and can accommodate a large group. If the hotel is expensive, you might want to reserve a block of rooms at another, less expensive motel as well. Then your guests have a choice. Before notifying guests of the specifics, verify your reservations. You will probably need to sign a contract with the motel, although a deposit shouldn't be required. You may also want to ask nearby friends to house guests who are unable to pay for a motel room.

WEDDING FLOWERS

Flowers are a wonderful way to tie colors and styles together and help set the tone for the wedding. Before you contract with a florist, look through their books of past events. Seeing what they have done will help you visualize

99

your wedding and determine what you want. When meeting with the florist, bring a color swatch of the bridesmaids' dresses to coordinate the flowers with the wedding colors.

Flowers can be very expensive, so prioritize what is most important about them—the color, the kind, the amount. Consider the time of year of your wedding. What will be available? Some winter weddings, for instance, use candles, wreaths, and greens instead of flowers. If a florist is too expensive, what about arranging flowers yourself? One recent bride visited florists for ideas but bought the flowers herself from a floral discount center. A roommate who had worked in a flower shop helped her to coordinate arrangements.

Some money-saving tips on floral decorations:

- Contact the church and see if there is another wedding on your day. If so, you could split the cost of some flowers or decorations if you and the other bride can agree to share the floral arrangements.
- Choose in-season flowers.
- Buy flowers from a discount floral center, and have friends help arrange them.
- Use more greens and fewer flowers.
- Use flowers from the church ceremony as the reception decorations.
- Have the reception site contract with a florist who may charge less than a regular florist.

THE REHEARSAL DINNER

The rehearsal dinner can be a wonderful time to applaud parents, relatives, and attendants with short anecdotes. A toast can be a wonderful way to thank friends and family for their investment in your lives. This is much easier than trying to squeeze your thanks into the wedding day. You may also want to use the rehearsal dinner as a time to reminisce, showing slides or videos of you and your groom.

Money-saving tips:

- Have the dinner in a home.
- Invite only parents, members of the wedding party, and their spouses.
- Make the decorations yourselves.

Typically the groom takes responsibility for this task, but you may decide to work together. Either way, begin planning several months prior to the trip. If you're using a travel agent, he will then have ample time to find the best rates on lodging, airfare, and other expenses. Some of the most popular honeymoon destinations are Hawaii; the Caribbean; the Virgin Islands; Orlando's Disney World; Miami Beach; the Florida Keys; the Poconos; San Francisco and Sonoma, California; Colorado Springs and Estes Park, Colorado. Of course, if your budget is tight, you may want to go to a special place close to home. One couple who were recent college graduates ended up at a peacock farm owned by family friends—noisy, but free!

Although you will probably be eager to start your honeymoon, we suggest you take a day after the wedding just to relax and unwind before you hop on a plane or jump in the car. And if possible, give yourself a few days after the honeymoon to recover and unpack before you head back to work.

Invitations should be addressed and mailed six to eight weeks before the wedding. They can be ordered from stationers, printers, gift and card stores, and catalogs. In addition, you can order response cards and a return envelope, or you may choose to have guests write out their own responses.

Carefully proofread invitations, response cards, and envelopes when the order is submitted, as well as when it is picked up. Traditionally the bride's parents issue the invitations and host the reception. However, you and your fiancé may issue the invitations, as can a close relative. Depending on your parents' marital status, there are several options for the wording of the invitation:

❦ Your mother and father can host.

❦ Your mother and stepfather can host.

❦ Your father and stepmother can host.

❦ Your divorced, unmarried, or widowed mother can host by herself.

❦ Your divorced, unmarried, or widowed father can host by himself.

- Divorced, unmarried parents can co-host.
- The groom's parents can host.
- The bride's parents and the groom's parents can co-host.
- Or the bride and groom can host the reception together.

Once the invitations arrive, address them by hand or use a professional calligrapher. Be sure to allow plenty of time for this. The outer envelope should have the guest's full name and title written out, as well as his town and state.

The inner envelope, if there is one, should have only the person's title and last name. The first names of children under sixteen, if they are invited, may be written on the inner envelope. Children over the age of sixteen should receive their own invitations. If a single friend is invited with a guest, the friend's name and "guest" ("Ms. Smith and guest") should be written on the inner envelope. The inner envelope always remains unsealed and is placed in the outer envelope so that the guest sees his name first (rather than the back of the envelope) when opening the invitation.

If the reception is some distance from the church, consider enclosing directions and a map, as well as information on the hotel reservations. Finally, make sure the entire invitation is weighed before postage is purchased. If reception cards, response cards, maps, and directions are enclosed, the envelope may be fairly heavy.

Money-saving ideas:
- Buy invitations at cost from a discount stationer.
- Order printed, rather than engraved, invitations.
- Have guests send in their own responses rather than supplying the response cards.
- Address the invitations yourself or with the help of friends.
- Design your own, creative invitations and have them printed.

GIFT REGISTRIES

Register early for gifts since this provides your guests ample time to shop, which is important if there are several pre-wedding parties or showers. You may want to set aside several hours to register so you will have plenty of time to choose patterns, colors, and cookware. If available, provide your parents and your fiancé's parents with the store's 800 number so they can give it to out-of-town guests inquiring about gift registries.

If you are planning to use professional musicians or a band, go hear them play, and review the music to be played at the wedding. If you are booking a deejay, it's wise to hear him also at an event. Discuss with him not only the music you want but what he will say. As an emcee at the reception, the deejay has regular access to a microphone—which can be a bonus or a liability. One deejay played the theme song from "Star Wars" as the bride and groom were introduced! Find out if the band and deejay have access to a cordless microphone, which can be valuable for toasts, particularly if the reception site is large.

If you decide to provide the music yourself, ask a friend or family member to bring stereo equipment and music, or have a friend emcee your event.

WEDDING CAKE

Now for some fun! Selecting and ordering the wedding cake is one of the most enjoyable parts of wedding planning, especially if you sample the many flavors available for both the cake and fillings. Order a cake that not only looks good but tastes good. Some brides choose different flavors for individual tiers on the cake. Many styles are available, depending on the number of guests you expect. Traditionally the top layer, or anniversary tier, is saved for the couple to freeze and eat on their first wedding anniversary.

If you want to decorate the cake with fresh flowers, coordinate this with the florist. He can provide a cake top and loose flowers for the rest of the cake. Cakes can be ordered from large bakeries, individuals working from their homes, friends, or caterers. At-home bakers tend to charge less. You might even have a

103

friend bake the cake if you're having a small wedding.

GROOM'S ATTIRE

To arrange for his own tuxedo as well as tuxedos for his groomsmen, the groom will need the measurements of all the ushers, his best man, and the father of the bride. If there's a ring bearer in the wedding, he should be dressed similarly to the groom or to the ushers. You may want to have a professional take measurements so you're sure they're accurate.

WEDDING RINGS

If you and your fiancé order rings, allow three to four weeks for arrival. Many brides and grooms have rings engraved with their names, initials, wedding date, or a favorite saying or verse. If you decide to do this, allow an additional week.

WEDDING TRANSPORTATION

You and your fiancé can discuss whether you would like a limousine, car, or horse and carriage. One young English doctor, Will Hamilton, hired a rag and bone man (junk collector) to arrive after the London ceremony with his horse and wagon to whisk him and his bride away! So use your ingenuity.

WEDDING PROGRAMS

A wedding program gives the order of worship for the ceremony, and it can be printed on plain paper or on program covers, which can be purchased from a local Christian bookstore or church. Some churches will print programs for a small fee, or local printers can typeset and copy them fairly quickly.

WEDDING FAVORS

Although favors are not required, they are a nice touch for each guest at the reception. Traditional ideas include:

- tulle bags filled with candy, Jordan almonds, or potpourri;
- small bags or boxes of chocolates (the bags can be tied with ribbon printed with

the bride's and groom's names, or the boxes can be custom printed);

- ❦ chocolate or white chocolate roses;
- ❦ chocolate mints with personalized foil;
- ❦ scented fabric flowers;
- ❦ chocolate spoons.

Money-saving tip:

- ❦ Buy the materials and candy, and assemble favors by hand.

DRESS FITTINGS

Finally. Your gorgeous dress has arrived and your wedding day is close at hand. As you begin fittings, you will be able to see—not just imagine—what you will look like as a bride. You and your bridesmaids should begin your fittings at least a month before the wedding.

The last month before the wedding is a glorious, but somewhat nerve-racking time. Guard your time. You will need time to yourself, time with your fiancé, time for last-minute details and decisions. In addition, there are many important things to wrap up.

MARRIAGE LICENSE

Marriage licenses should be obtained in the state in which the wedding is taking place. Some states require blood tests; others do not. The license must be used within a certain period of time after it has been granted, so verify that the wedding falls within that time.

SEATING AND PLACE CARDS

If the reception is a sit-down meal, you will probably have to wait until several weeks before the wedding, when most of the responses are in, to create a seating chart. Reserve an evening or two to place guests at various tables. Once this is finished, place cards with table numbers can be written out for all of the guests. Some things to consider:

- ❦ How many people will sit at the head table?
- ❦ Will all of your attendants sit with you?
- ❦ Will spouses and dates sit with attendants?
- ❦ How large will the family table(s) be?
- ❦ Who will sit in the tables closest to you?
- ❦ With whom should single friends or solo guests sit?

105

❦ If your parents are divorced, how close should they sit to each other?

If several guests have not responded but may come anyway, make place cards for them. If they don't come, it's not a problem, and if they do, they will feel welcome.

DIRECTIONS TO EVENTS

Print extra copies of the directions and have them waiting at the church. Many guests forget to bring directions with them and are grateful for another copy. You may also need to provide information on where to park at the reception if it's not readily apparent. Also, at the rehearsal provide the wedding party with written directions to the rehearsal dinner site, if necessary.

FOLLOW UP WITH SERVICE PROVIDERS

It is essential to follow up with service providers one or two weeks before the wedding. For the reception and rehearsal dinner this is easy; the balance of the bill is usually paid one to two weeks prior to the events anyway. However,

for safety's sake you or your mother should call *everyone*—the caterer, musicians, deejay, bakery, reception and rehearsal dinner sites, photographer, videographer, florist, limousine service, and hotels—to verify that all is in place. By doing this you avoid the stress of having an essential player fail to show up because of a misunderstanding over time or place.

One bride called her videographer a week before the wedding only to discover she had never been placed on his schedule! After hyperventilating for a few minutes, she tracked down a record of her deposit and the signed contract, and the company was required to supply someone to tape her wedding.

During your follow-up, touch base with the banquet manager or catering manager who is hosting the reception. In most cases they require a final head count and payment before the reception. When figuring the final number, allow for the fact that some people who have said they are coming will not, and some who have said they are not coming may indeed show up. As a precaution, ask the catering manager how many unexpected meals he can provide if the head count is off.

Ask all service providers who will actually be a part of the wedding (photographer, deejay, videographer) to wear a dark suit or tuxedo. Most do anyway, but this will prevent someone from showing up in tennis shoes and shorts.

OTHER LAST-MINUTE DETAILS

A number of details may wait until the end: packing, moving boxes to your new home, purchasing gifts for your wedding party and groom. As much as possible, keep the week before the wedding free because things will come up.

Try to take some time off from work before the wedding, even if it's only a few days. A day or two before the wedding, steal away with your fiancé for a few hours alone!

And on your wedding day? Designate a troubleshooter to deal with last-minute logistics and problems that inevitably arise, even if you have to pay a friend or relative to do so.

This will ease the burden from your mother and relieve you of some worries.

The Most Important Element of All: Your Ceremony

In the midst of all the planning, details, coordination, decisions, and people, we encourage you not to lose sight of the most important element of all—the actual wedding ceremony. Whatever type of wedding you choose to have, use it to honor God and your parents, and to reflect the love you feel for each other.

The music you choose will create the mood of your wedding. Certain pieces like Mendelssohn's "Wedding March," Wagner's "Bridal Chorus," and Clarke's "Trumpet Voluntary" are always popular. In addition to these stately compositions, "Jesu, Joy of Man's Desiring" by Johann Sebastian Bach, Pachelbel's "Canon in D," and Handel's "Air" and "Allegro Maestro" are wedding favorites.[1]

Passages from the Old and New Testaments can be meaningful additions to the ceremony. Which are best? Ask your minister for those he recommends, or look up "marriage," "love," "man," or "woman" in a Bible concordance to find verses that convey a special message to you. Once you have located the passages, find a translation you like—one that has beautiful prose but is understandable as well. Some favorite passages for brides and grooms include:[2]

❦ Genesis 2:18–24: "Then the LORD God said, 'It is not good that man should be alone; I will make him a helper as his partner.'"

❦ Ephesians 5:22–23: "Wives, be subject to your husbands as you are to the Lord. For the husband is the head of the wife, just as Christ is the head of the church."

❦ 1 Corinthians 13:4–8: "Love is patient, love is kind; love is not envious or boastful or arrogant or rude. It does not insist on its own way; it is not irritable or resentful; it does not rejoice in wrongdoing, but rejoices in the truth. It bears all things, believes all things, hopes all things, endures all things. Love never ends."

In addition to appropriate music and scriptures, we believe your wedding will be even more meaningful if, in some fashion, you honor your parents. You might elect to have your fathers read scripture and your mothers light individual candles (you and your groom can later light the unity candle together). You may also want to honor your mothers at the end of the ceremony by giving each a rose. Some brides and grooms choose to give a rose and a kiss to their new mothers-in-law.

As you and your fiancé begin your life together, don't lose sight of the power of the commitment you are making. Your honesty and vulnerability in your vows and comments to each other will touch your friends and loved ones deeply and give them a window into your relationship. While your guests will appreciate a well-executed production, they will long remember a chance to see your heart.

Chapter Nine

CREATING A LOVE
THAT LASTS

Many waters cannot quench love,

neither can floods drown it.

SONG OF SOLOMON 8:7

The Washington Post reported that actress Penelope Ann Miller filed for divorce on January 18, 1995. The thirty-one-year-old actress had just married William Emerson Arnett on December 9, but apparently the couple developed "irreconcilable differences" during their forty-day, ill-fated marriage.[1]

Ah, for a love that lasts. Centuries ago the apostle Paul, who never married, wrote one of the most beautiful and timeless pieces on love: "Love… bears all things, believes all things, hopes all things, endures all things. Love never ends" (1 Corinthians 13:4–8). In those words Paul captured the longing of our human hearts for a love that stands the test of time.

As you and your fiancé plan your wedding, no doubt you feel your love will endure for a lifetime. Even in an era of widespread divorce, why go into marriage believing anything else? But how can you guarantee you will still be together in fifteen or twenty years? *Time* magazine states that in 1993, 2.3 million couples "performed the most optimistic of human rituals and got married. That same year, 1.2 million couples agreed, officially, that their marriages could not be saved. Again in 1993, the Bureau of the Census projected that four out of ten first marriages would end in divorce."[2] Obviously, sheer optimism is not enough.

Neither is the fire, the heat, of sexual passion.

This past weekend my husband and I celebrated our twentieth wedding anniversary at the gracious, old Williamsburg Inn in colonial Williamsburg, Virginia. In our large and lovely room, furnished with reproductions of British antiques, a fire had been carefully laid. As we munched on cheese and crackers, Don grew philosophical. Knowing that I love the burst of flame and crackle when the kindling first catches fire, he mused, "A fire is like a marriage. At first it's thrilling and intense, but the flames die down when the logs catch fire. At this point the fire looks less dramatic, but its heat is

The vows you make to each other will be impossible to keep unless you make Christ the third partner in your marriage.

❦

even greater. And later when all that's left are the burning coals, that's when the fire is hottest yet."

As we reflected on our marriage, we agreed that some of the drama and thrill had been replaced over the years by a quieter love—memories of a shared life together, companionship, joint accomplishments. And our love persists, not as a burst of intense flame, but as enduring logs and embers.

BRENDA

How can you ensure your marital fire will last? Only through commitment to each other, for better and for worse. And how can you keep this lifetime commitment? Only with God's help. He alone gives us the power to remain true to our commitments. Lon Solomon, senior minister at the McLean Bible Church in McLean, Virginia, says that when he performs weddings he tells couples, "You are entering the most difficult relationship on the face of this earth to make work. The vows you make to each other today will be impossible to keep unless you make Christ the third partner in your marriage."

What does it mean to make Christ your marriage partner? To do so is to acknowledge that no matter how wise or compassionate you are, you simply aren't smart enough, kind enough, or forgiving enough to be the husband or wife you need to be. No one is. All of us need God to soften our hearts when we get angry, to dissolve our pride when we don't want to say we're sorry, and to give us hope when we're disillusioned and discouraged.

Who is better able to school us in the disciplines of marriage than God? After all, He created marriage in the first place, in the garden of Eden. And Christ's first miracle was at the wedding in Cana where he turned the water into wine so His host wouldn't be embarrassed and so the bride and groom could revel in their wedding celebration. Since marriage is a sacred event, it's critical that we understand how God views marriage and the importance He places on marital commitment.

God's View of Marriage

When Adam and Eve were joined together in Genesis 2, their relationship was described in almost mystical terms. Eve became "bone" of Adam's bone and "flesh of his flesh." One—indivisible souls. No longer were they merely separate bodies, minds, and personalities; instead they were able to achieve a oneness

that defies explanation. Like Adam and Eve, when we marry, we are also given the ability to experience a oneness unmatched in any other relationship. We have the gift of enjoying both sexual and emotional intimacy in the confines of a committed, sacrosanct relationship. Granted, we are still individuals with separate personalities and personal histories. But that longing each has for deep union with another is only possible to achieve in marriage.

But to experience true intimacy, we must first leave home. Genesis 2:24 says, "Therefore a man leaves his father and his mother and clings to his wife, and they become one flesh." It's not enough to leave our parental home physically. That's the easy part. One must also leave psychologically. This leaving and cleaving is key to achieving oneness in marriage. A woman who remains emotionally dependent on her parents siphons off emotional energy and intimacy from her husband. The same is true for a husband. To continue to look to a parent for primary comfort and advice is to refuse to transfer one's dependency needs to a

Like Adam and Eve, when we marry,

we are also given the ability to experience a oneness

unmatched in any other relationship.

❧

partner. Therapists who work with couples know that the man or woman who has never left home emotionally cannot experience genuine intimacy. He or she remains a child, merely playing at the game of marriage.

The Differing Roles We Play

In addition to providing the opportunity for intimacy in marriage, God has also established unique roles for a husband and wife. Ed Satterfield, a minister at McLean Presbyterian Church in McLean, Virginia, instructs couples to take seriously the gifts and responsibilities each has to contribute to a balanced relation-

ship. As the minister at Greg and Kristen's wedding, he charged them with the following:

Greg, I charge you as a Christian husband:

First, to bring to this marriage security. This means that you make Kristen feel safe with you. Find ways to demonstrate your love for her. Show her that above all other persons she is first in your life. Security means that you work hard at causing Kristen to realize how important she is to you. Show her in concrete ways how much you value her and how great is her value to others. It means that you take time to listen—putting all else aside—that you take time to show sincere appreciation for her gifts to you, and that you take time to give her affection. Look for ways to build her up. Kristen needs to know your love and commitment. Give to her security.

Second, bring to this marriage leadership. God gives you that distinct role in this relationship. Leadership does not mean you make all the decisions without regard for Kristen's feelings or opinions. Being the leader means you seek a clear sense of God's direction. Know what He wants for your lives, what are His standards for your character and conduct. Then make sure you and Kristen get there. Leadership is watching over the spiritual life of the home. Make sure both of you are growing to love Christ more each year. Develop strong convictions based upon God's Word so that your life is characterized by the quality of life and purpose inherent in being a Christian.

Greg, these are your charges: security and leadership. May God grant you grace to enable you to be what He desires you to be as a Christian husband.

Kristen, I charge you as a Christian wife: First, to bring to this marriage encouragement. One of the most vital needs Greg has is to know he is significant. Show him you respect him and that you believe in him. It is easy to criticize, but hard to affirm. Know Greg's strengths and remind him continually of what he does well and what is good in him. He needs, as will the rest of your family, to know you are behind him all the way. Find ways to build him up. Give encouragement.

Second, bring to this marriage peace. Find ways you can care for the emotional climate of the home. We all desire and need peace. Our homes are a place where we come for rest. Make your home a place that is restful. Be creative in watching over your family life. Bring to it order; develop in it a positive atmosphere. Make it a place of support and caring, of listening and sharing. God has uniquely equipped you to watch over these things. Develop a deep trust and hope in Christ and then labor hard to create in your marriage relationship and in your family life the quality of confidence in God.

Kristen, these are your charges: encouragement and peace. May God grant you grace to enable you to be what He wants you to be as a Christian wife.

May God bless you both in this pursuit to have a strong marriage. May your relationship demonstrate to all that God is alive and true because your marriage is unique in its love and strength. The Lord Jesus Christ is the third partner in your marriage. May you always recognize and give Him His proper place in your life together.

Making and Keeping Vows

As you stand together on your wedding day, you too will hear the priest or minister charge you with your new responsibilities as a husband and wife. And you will speak timeless and beautiful vows to each other, committing to fulfill those responsibilities: "Will you take this man to be your lawfully wedded husband? Will you, forsaking all others, keep only unto him, so long as you both shall live?" Whatever language you and your fiancé choose for your vows, you will make binding commitments to each other before God and His community, commitments to be lived out day after day.

Yet few of us in the late twentieth century realize the enormous significance of these vows made to the Lord. God taught the ancient Israelites that even rash or foolish vows were significant and needed to be kept or forgiven (Leviticus 5:4). Numbers 30:2 states, "When a man makes a vow to the LORD, or swears an oath to bind himself by a pledge, he shall not break his word; he shall do according to all that proceeds out of his mouth." According to this passage, women were also bound by their spoken vows, and only their husbands could nullify them.

Though no one is forced to make a vow, once made, a vow binds us in heaven and on earth. In Moses' day, and in our own, promises made to God and to others are to be kept, even if that proves costly. Marital vows are broken at great consequence, as anyone who has ever experienced divorce knows. Because of the

115

ongoing pain of divorce, it's not surprising that God admonishes men by saying, "Do not let anyone be faithless to the wife of his youth. For I hate divorce, says the LORD, the God of Israel.... So take heed to yourselves and do not be faithless" (Malachi 2:15–16).

Marriage-Saving

How can you and your fiancé best prepare to keep your vows, even before you say "I do"? Now is the time to think seriously about what you will pledge to each other before God and His witnesses.

To ensure that a couple takes their commitments seriously, there's a growing movement in this country called "marriage-saving."[3] Increasingly, churches of all denominations are requiring couples to have premarital counseling before their wedding day. In some twenty-seven cities—ranging from Louisville, Kentucky, to Modesto, California—clergy have drafted a marriage policy that requires couples to prepare for marriage a full six months prior to their wedding day. And if they refuse? The clergy in this marriage-saving program will not perform the wedding within their churches. This may sound harsh, but in all likelihood this stand will, in the long run, foster stronger marriages.[4]

Laura Richards and Mark Geyman took a serious look at the demands of marriage as participants in a marriage preparation program at St. Augustine Catholic Church in Jeffersonville, Indiana. Working with an older mentoring couple, John and Patti Thompson, Laura and Mark were part of the marriage-saving program. When Laura and Mark first made plans for a June wedding, they were riding high on sheer euphoria. But then Patti began to question them about their deeper fears, Laura's jealousy, their worry about in-laws. Through premarital counseling with these veterans of a thirty-one-year marriage, Laura and Mark began their marriage on a stronger base.[5]

Across America, many Protestant and Catholic churches offer premarital counseling courses, which stress the sexual aspects of marriage, finances, communication, and relationships with in-laws. In addition, the Catholic church offers weekend retreats for engaged couples called Catholic Engaged Encounter. This nondenominational program grew out of Marriage Encounter and is run by volunteer couples. Mary Ellen McCormick, along with her husband, Peter, leads four retreats yearly. She says, "The weekend provides an opportunity for a couple to pull away from frantic wedding planning for forty-eight hours to focus on their relationship."

During the retreat a couple not only hears two couples and a priest discuss communication, family relationships, sex, fears, and spirituality, but they write revealing love letters to each other. In addition, the couple meets other couples and often forges lasting friendships. Mary Ellen, who does follow-up work with the attendees, confirms the divorce rate is quite low for these couples. "In eleven years," she says, "only once have I heard of a couple separating."

Spiritual Housecleaning

In addition to premarital counseling and courses, spiritual housecleaning is an essential preparation for your wedding day. What we don't work out, we act out, especially in our intimate relationships. If we have any grievances or bitterness toward parents, friends, siblings, or others, we need to address these so we don't act out the pain, anger, or mistrust in our new marriages. This is especially true if we hold grudges against the parent of the opposite sex. The groom who holds a grudge against his mother will carry some of that anger and mistrust into his relationship with his wife. Conversely, the bride who feels rejected by her father will find her perceptions of her husband colored by this relationship. So we are wise to recognize our feelings and try to forgive those who have hurt us before we marry.

117

Contrary to the old movie *Love Story,* being in love *does* mean we have to say we're sorry. Again and again. And it also means we have to forgive and ask to be forgiven on occasion. In fact, forgiveness is essential for marriage and for our mental health. God, who made us, tells us forgiveness is not an option. Any wrong others have done to us is small change compared to the huge debt we owe God.

In Matthew 18 Jesus tells us we are to forgive others seventy times over. Then he tells the story of a king who wishes to settle accounts with his slaves. One slave owes him ten thousand talents (about 150 years worth of wages). The slave cannot pay his debt and begs for mercy. The king, out of compassion for his servant, forgives the debt. Then the slave goes out and sees a peer who owes him one hundred denarii (about 100 days wages). Even though the fellow slave pleads for mercy, the hard-hearted slave has the audacity to have his debtor thrown into prison.

When the king later hears this, he is outraged. He calls the first slave in and says, "You wicked slave! I forgave you all that debt because you pleaded with me. Should you not have had mercy on your fellow slave, as I had mercy on you?" (18:32–33). Then he hands the unforgiving slave over to torturers until he pays his entire debt. Jesus says, "So my heavenly Father will also do to every one of you, if you do not forgive your brother or sister from your heart" (18:35).

These are strong words. Yet the message is clear. The debt we owe God for our sinful thoughts and actions far surpasses any debt that another can ever owe us. We are commanded to forgive injuries we've suffered in order to receive mercy for our huge indebtedness to God. To be forgiven, we must first forgive.

For those who have violated their consciences in past relationships, the engagement period is a time to seek and grant forgiveness, to wipe the slate clean spiritually.

A thirty-two-year-old accountant spent several months dealing with the effects of his sexual past on his fiancée, who was a virgin. As they talked into the wee hours of the morning about his past relationships, Brad could see the pain his earlier actions had caused Joy. And as they approached their wedding day, both grew apprehensive that the groomsmen, who had known Brad during his freewheeling days, would bring up his past on their wedding day—a day Brad and Joy wished to symbolize a new beginning. To counter this, Brad wrote the following letter which he gave to each of his groomsmen after the frivolities of the rehearsal dinner.

Gentlemen:

I wanted to write you a letter to tell you what this wedding means to me. I always knew I wanted to get married, but I never thought there could be so much to love about one person. Joy means the world to me. She is truly a precious gift from God. She is exactly that—a gift from God.

In the last few years the Lord has drawn me closer to Himself and has shown me many things. One thing He has let me know is the true meaning of the word beauty through Joy. I never understood this before. Now I know.

God has not only taught me about beauty through the woman I love, but He has shown me where I went wrong. I have definite regrets about some of the things I did in my teens and twenties. These acts have caused much pain in my relationship with Joy, and I now wish I had those decisions to make all over again. I have changed. My views, desires, and feelings have changed. My first two concerns now are God and Joy (in that order). I will do whatever I have to do to keep myself out of situations that dishonor God and Joy. I will also do my best to do the things that honor God and Joy. God has opened my eyes to what is true and important. I know I will continue to change as He opens my eyes further.

My marriage to Joy is a one-time deal. I don't want to attempt marriage without God in the center; I don't want to go through another day without God guiding me. This is who I am now. The love that Joy and I share is from God and I hope you see this tomorrow. Thanks for being a part of this special day!

Love, Brad

As it turned out, Brad's groomsmen honored the tone he and Joy longed to establish for their wedding. Amid all of the celebration and the rousing toasts, there were no sexual innuendoes or references to Brad's past. Instead, several of the groomsmen offered warm, moving tributes to their longtime, treasured friend of dodge ball days.

Christianity and Your Marriage

What are some of the benefits of creating a strong spiritual foundation for your marriage? Psychiatrist David Larson and medical researcher Mary Ann Mayo report that people who attend church even once a month increase their chances of staying married.[6] According to Larson and Mayo, "Christianity provides support for married couples to be committed, to show respect, to be emotionally supportive, to communicate effectively, and creates a stable power structure for the home.

This intimacy solidifies a marriage romantically and sexually."[7]

Larson and Mayo reviewed a host of scientific studies and found that the woman who goes to church regularly and takes her faith seriously has greater sexual satisfaction than the one who does not. Who would ever have considered religion to be an aphrodisiac? Yet according to Larson and Mayo, "The most religious women were most satisfied with the frequency of intercourse and felt free to discuss sex openly with their husbands, and, most surprisingly, were more orgasmic than were the nonreligious."[8]

And that's not all. In addition to marital satisfaction, you and your future husband are likely to live longer if you have a personal, deeply satisfying religious faith. According to Dr. Larson, studies show that churchgoers have less risk of heart disease, lower blood pressure, and are hospitalized far less often than those who don't attend church.[9]

So it doesn't pay, either sexually or physically, to ignore the spiritual aspects of your marriage. In fact, a marriage without the nurture of God's love is like a tree with shallow roots. For a season the tree may blossom and lift its branches upward, but when the rains come, the winds blow, and the hail assails its branches, the tree will list. It may even fall to the ground.

The key, then, is to create a union with deep roots. A love that lasts.

A Love that Endures

Marty, a fifty-four-year-old Spanish teacher with fiery red hair, has been married to Elliott Larson, an internist in Southborough, Massachusetts, for twenty-eight years. Despite her parents' painful divorce when she was twelve, Marty tells her friends that she and Elliott have had "a wonderful life." Their secret? "God has influenced our lives every day," says this mother of five sons.

Former missionaries, Elliott and Marty have experienced God's love and care in some far-flung places. After years in Washington,

D.C. the couple moved to Afghanistan, to London, England, and then to Southborough, where they are deeply involved in the local L'Abri Fellowship, a Christian study center.

Marty and Elliott believe that Christianity has been the core of their daily lives and their marriage. Each morning they read the Bible and pray together. Over the years as Elliott has practiced medicine and Marty has homeschooled their sons, they have felt God's steady influence and care in their lives. Marty reminisces about one time when God was especially close.

The year was 1974. Marty and Elliott had just been ordered out of Afghanistan because the government erroneously believed that Elliott, who taught in the medical school in Kabul, was a CIA agent. As they anxiously packed their meager possessions and two young sons, ages two and five, into a Volkswagen sedan, they headed for the Iranian border. Three hours into Iran, having driven on washboard roads, they heard a loud noise. The Volkswagen's engine sputtered and died. "It was a bleak and terrifying moment," says Elliott. "We were surrounded by miles of sand, sparse vegetation, and no sign of human life. We prayed, and soon an old tanker came by. The driver couldn't tow us, but he left us a rope." Feeling somewhat desperate, Marty and Elliott prayed again. Within the hour, a heavy Jeep drove up and agreed to tow them to Kerman, a town seventy miles away.

"The boys and I rode in the Jeep," Marty states, "drinking Coke and eating fresh dates. That night, we slept in the home of a stranger, an Iranian pastor. He and his Australian wife took us in for a whole week while our car was being repaired." How did they feel about this experience? "Immensely reassured," says Marty. "At a time when we felt rejected, God took care of us. And weeks later, when we finally arrived in England, Elliott found a superb job."

Flash forward to August 1994. Marty and Elliott return to England, this time to attend the wedding of their blond, twenty-two-year-old son, Mark, to Su. Recent graduates of Cambridge University, the young couple asked Elliott to give the wedding sermon. Gladly he assumed the role of pastor and spoke of Christ as the standard for human love, quoting as his text for that morning, "Just as I have loved you, you also should love one another" (John 13:34). What he and Marty believed and had experienced, Elliott passed on to the next generation.

Whether your parents or your fiancé's parents have given you a spiritual legacy or not, you can be the new generation that honors God on your wedding day and in your daily life. If you do, you and your husband will have something rich and deep to pass on to your children. Remember what Jackson Pollock said to Eric Liddell in the movie *Chariots of Fire,* "He who honors God, God will honor." That applies to marriage as well as running a race for Olympic gold.

Chapter Ten

SAVING THE
BEST FOR LAST

Do not arouse or awaken love until it so desires.

SONG OF SOLOMON 3:5, NIV

When Craig Blackman married Joette Zieverink in 1990, he was thirty-one and she was thirty-four. Both were virgins. Craig, a champion athlete who wrestled in Eastern Europe with his college team, was inducted into the Franklin Marshall Hall of Fame shortly before their wedding. Joette stood proudly that day as she and Craig's family watched him stride onto the football field at half-time. She, a television producer for the Christian Broadcasting Network, remembers that both of their mothers had prayed for years for them to meet and someday marry the right person.

When Craig and Joette realized they loved each other and wanted to marry, they decided to save sex for marriage. "We wanted sex to be our wedding gift to each other," says Joette. "We both believed sex was a sacred gift, and we thought it was wonderful that we were still pure in that respect, that we didn't have a lot of baggage to work through."

Was it hard for this modern couple to wait? "It was very difficult to be chaste during our engagement," said Joette. "After all, Craig and I had our own apartments and lots of opportunities for sex. But we had close, engaged friends, and all four of us kept each other accountable. Also, we knew that if we didn't wait, it would impair our personal relationship with God and with each other."

As Craig and Joette stood facing each other on their wedding day, they held hands and spoke from the heart. In words that touched many guests deeply, each said to the other, "I have waited for you for years."

What a gift—to love with restraint and devotion. It's never easy. To be in love is to desire sexual union with the one we love. An old Italian proverb captures truth: "He who is not impatient is not in love." As a result of changing cultural mores and sexual pressures, many men and women decide not to postpone sexual intimacy until after marriage. But others elect to wait. Whether you have waited for sex or not, this chapter is for you. Our intention is twofold: to present the biblical perspective on sexuality and to challenge you to think about chastity and its rewards.

What Does the Bible Say about Sex?

First Corinthians 6:18 states, "Flee from sexual immorality. All other sins a man commits are outside his body, but he who sins sexually sins against his own body" (NIV). Scripture warns that the consequences of sexual immorality invade our very being—our bodies and hearts. The Bible clearly acknowledges that having sex is more than just a physical act; rather, sexual intercourse involves the body, mind, and heart. All. This is particularly true for women, who cannot divorce sexual intercourse from its emotional components. And three decades of casual sex with the attendant media hoopla haven't changed this basic gender difference. If you doubt this, ask any therapist who works with women and seeks to help them with their romantic relationships.

Recognizing that we are multifaceted beings, God created sex to take place within the psychological and legal safety of marriage. Marriage is the only suitable context for the total vulnerability sexual intimacy ushers in. Notwithstanding the current prevalence of divorce, marriage is meant to be an enduring institution. Only in marriage can a man and woman be physically intimate and psychologically naked as well. Because of the vows both make, a man and woman can count on each other to be there tomorrow. If marital vows are honored and kept, marriage provides a guarantee no other relationship can offer.

What Is Real Intimacy?

What most of us desire, but few experience, is genuine intimacy with another person. Psychologists define intimacy as the ability to be close to another in a committed relationship—to be transparent and authentic without the fear of rejection. It's the bedrock ability to trust another person with your heart and soul, to share your deepest self, knowing you will be loved and accepted as you are. While marriage doesn't guarantee this level of intimacy and acceptance, it does create an environment where this can occur. All those promises—that commitment before God and His community—can foster emotional security and create an intimate and safe place.

How Do We Learn to Be Intimate?

How do we develop true intimacy with another person? We meet; the magic begins. We observe, circling each other in a wary dance that grows faster and more intense over time. We share our thoughts, feelings, and vulnerabilities as we scan the face we are beginning to love. We wait to see how our revelations will be received. As we share "the issues of the heart," we move closer to each other.

The challenge of the engagement, then, is to become guardians of each other's hearts—to trust each other with our increasingly vulnerable selves. If we become sexually intimate too soon, we short-circuit this progression.

It's a whole lot tougher to explore the sometimes hidden terrain of feelings and dreams than it is to explore each other's bodies. One thirty-nine-year-old lawyer grinned and said, "If a man gets sexually involved with a woman, he gets distracted from his primary task—getting to know her: who she is, what she thinks and feels, and what she needs from him."

The fact is, some of us grew up without being emotionally close to our parents. For us, dismantling our walls and learning to trust is hard work. We need all the empathy and patience we can get. As the intimacy experts for both sexes, women are generally more comfortable than men with the language of feelings and the heart. So if a woman wants to really know her man and have him know her heart, she and he need to put the brakes on sexually. Besides, a woman may feel guilty and exploited if she goes against her conscience. Even if she doesn't engage in intercourse, if she gives more of her body than she feels comfortable giving, once she marries, she may feel violated or disappointed and have sexual problems during the first year.

To experience sex at its best, we need to build genuine heart-to-heart, soul-to-soul intimacy before we jump into bed with each other. As we bare our souls, as we learn to pray together and hold each other accountable before God, then we experience true intimacy. If we do this, we will discover after marriage that the sexual experience is intensified, untainted by guilt, boredom, or banality.

When a couple saves sex for marriage, sex becomes the symbolic and physical expression of their connection on all other levels—intellectual, emotional, spiritual. Now one flesh, their bodies no longer belong exclusively to themselves but to each other.

First Corinthians 7:4 expresses this concept beautifully: "The wife's body does not belong to her alone but also to her husband. In the same way, the husband's body does not belong to him alone but also to his wife" (NIV). Our bodies, then, become consummate gifts we give each other in holy matrimony.

During their marriage of four and a half years, Craig and Joette believe they are enjoying the fruits of waiting. Now the parents of three-year-old Brooke—a beautiful, articulate little girl—both feel they can trust each other to be faithful, in great measure, because they waited. "We used the word 'covenant' in our sacred vows," remarks Joette, "because we wanted to affirm that we were totally committed to each other."

But What If You Haven't Waited?

If you and your fiancé haven't saved sex for marriage, you may already be struggling with guilt and sadness. Perhaps you're thinking, "What about me? My fiancé and I are sexually involved. We can't go back, so what do we do now?"

If you feel like you've blown it, take heart. While you can't change what has happened, you can reclaim your chastity from this

When a couple saves sex for marriage, sex becomes the symbolic and physical expression of their connection on all other levels—intellectual, emotional, spiritual.

moment on. Even if you had other sexual relationships and are sexually involved with your fiancé, you can choose to save sex, from this point on, for marriage. Of course, abstinence will be tough, and you can only do this for something more compelling and ultimately more rewarding than immediate gratification. When you agree to postpone the sexual celebration of your union, you acknowledge that something is different after marriage.

Besides, think of what you'll miss if you don't abstain. What can be more disappointing on your wedding night than to realize that you've saved nothing for marriage, that you've sacrificed your spiritual and emotional growth before marriage for sexual pleasure? Delaying sexual gratification will help you

mature and learn to practice self-control in other areas of life. So if you are currently involved, we challenge you to put the brakes on sexually and explore the various facets of each other's personalities.

What will help you and your fiancé abstain from sex? First, you need to come to God, confess your sin, and ask Him to help you recover your personal purity. First John 1:9 is clear: "If we confess our sins, he who is faithful and just will forgive us our sins and cleanse us from all unrighteousness." You can do an about face and be forgiven for your past. As you and your fiancé create or restore fellowship with God, He will prove faithful and give you both strength to resist sexual temptation. Scripture states, "God is faithful, and he will not let you be tested beyond your strength, but with the testing he will also provide the way out so that you may be able to endure it" (1 Corinthians 10:13). And if you fail? Try again. With God's help you can abstain.

To be chaste on your wedding day, you both need to break free from your past. How? You may want to talk this through with a counselor. And you may decide to tell your fiancé about your past. Some counselors might not advise sharing past experiences, so you will need to weigh this carefully. We feel it is possible to tell the truth broadly and thus create a relationship based on mutual trust and honesty.

If you choose to tell your fiancé about earlier relationships, spare the details; they can only cause him unnecessary pain, and they're hard to forget. Never, never lie or withhold essential information, and don't provide information in installments. No sequels. No second acts. This only undermines the fledgling trust you're working to create. Being open and honest will allow both of you to confront the past, deal with your emotions

(all the anger and sadness), and put the past behind you.

You Waited, He Didn't

If, on the other hand, you have been chaste but your fiancé has a sexual past, you may feel hurt and disappointed when you learn his truth. After all, you waited for him. Denise describes hearing about her fiancé's past as "gut-wrenching." She says, "I felt betrayed. I had waited for years for the man I would someday marry. Why didn't he wait for me?"

John's attitude toward his past ultimately enabled Denise to put it behind her. "John cried when he told me about his former relationships. Once he became a Christian, which was shortly before we began dating, he began to see his past in a new light. As I listened to him struggle to be honest, I was forced to look at areas in my own life where I had missed the mark. The fact that John was truly sorry was the only thing that helped me move on. If he

129

❦

had said, 'I didn't do anything wrong,' our relationship would have ended."

And if both of you have sown wild oats? You and your fiancé will need to deal with this head-on. Earlier sexual relationships may produce ghosts in the bedroom, performance anxiety or competitiveness, and difficulties with trust. Jenna and Paul, both in their early thirties, had had prior lovers when they met. Once they decided to marry, they chose to tell each other about earlier relationships. "I had no idea my past would make Paul feel so insecure," says Jenna, "or that he would find it hard to trust me. After all, he had his own story. It took us months to work through our baggage." If you haven't confronted this prior to engagement, deal with your past as early in the engagement as possible.

If you both can forgive and move on, commit to breaking free from the past. Using past transgressions as a weapon in later fights or disagreements is unfair. In *Building Your Mate's Self-Esteem,* Dennis and Barbara Rainey emphasize the importance of letting the past go. "One woman had been in a dating relationship she knew was not right. She and her boyfriend had experimented sexually. Finally she broke off the relationship. During the year that ensued, Isaiah 43:18–19 became very real to her: 'Do not call to mind the former things, or ponder things of the past. Behold, I will do something new, now it will spring forth; will you not be aware of it? I will even make a roadway in the wilderness, rivers in the desert'" (NASB).[1] Loving always means forgiving and moving on. British actor and writer Peter Ustinov once said, "Love is an act of endless forgiveness, a tender look which becomes a habit."[2]

Even though you may forgive each other, don't expect to forget instantly. Cheryl, whose husband was sexually promiscuous before he became a Christian, said it took her a long time to forget the other women and begin to feel like number one. She felt her husband's former lovers were ghosts in the bedroom for some time. What helped? Her husband's refusal to discuss details of his earlier relationships and the fact that he said, again and again, "Remember, I chose to marry you!"

Setting Limits or How Can You Make It to the Honeymoon?

So how do you deal with sexual temptation in your current relationship? If you or your fiancé has been sexually active in prior relationships, set limits early in your relationship. Susan, who married a man with a sexual past, says, "If one of you has been sexually active, it will be harder to set limits in your current relationship, but it's even more important. Not only will it set a strong precedent for trust in marriage, but it will help both of you see this relationship as different from all others. As unique and special." About setting limits, she adds, "Common-sense helps. Matt and I never took trips alone together, although we would have liked to. I've seen unmarried couples go away together, thinking their standards will carry them through. That's just inviting trouble. Spending time in public settings and restaurants rather than in our empty apartments helped too." Also, it's important during the stressful times to get enough rest. When you're tired, your defenses are down.

Great Expectations: The Wedding Night and Honeymoon

At long last. The wedding is finally over and you're alone in your hotel room. What happens next belongs uniquely to you and the love of your life. If you've waited, sexual tension will be at its height. One twenty-eight-year-old groom possessed bedroom eyes as he watched his bride walk down the aisle. It was obvious to the middle-aged, graying guests that this groom had one thing on his mind. And at their dinner dance, as he whispered to his bride and stroked her hand, her face, or encircled her waist with his arm, he appeared all too eager for the festivities to end.

And if you've regained chastity over a period of weeks or months? Even then anticipation builds and a resurgence of passion can occur. One couple who stopped having sex a month before their wedding said they "built up so much anticipation that the night turned out to be very passionate."[3]

Savoring the Best at Last

We hope your wedding night will be the beginning of a sexually fulfilling marriage.

Although this is not a sex manual, and we are not sex therapists, we want to share some insights. We'll leave the specifics to you.

Be gentle with each other. No matter how amorous you are, you will be very, very tired. And you'll probably be hungry, having eaten little all day. So take care of your needs for sustenance, a gentle massage, as well as romance. Think of room service or ask a friend to pack a basket of edibles to take along with you.

Understand that no matter how much you plan to do other things on your wedding night, sexual consummation is the first act of marital love. Joe and Linda discussed their wedding night well in advance. They agreed to go to their hotel room after the reception to unwind, to talk, and to reflect on their wedding day. Because the reception lasted longer than expected, Linda was unable to change from her wedding dress before leaving. As a result, she wore her gown to the hotel room and needed Joe's help to take it off. "That was it!" laughs Linda. "So much for our good intentions!"

Only in marriage can a man and woman be physically intimate and psychologically naked as well.

❧

Whether sex on your wedding night is glorious, or simply pleasant and comfortable, what's important is that you have this window of time to explore each other's bodies and begin to learn what gives each other sexual pleasure. Few of us know all we need to know about sex at the time we marry, and we certainly don't know all we need to know about what gives our partner pleasure. Only over the course of many years together does sex become perfected. And even then—only if we deepen our emotional connection with each other day by day, year by year. So if your wedding night has its glitches, laugh together and understand that you have a lot to learn, particularly if you're virgins. But what better person to create this sexual bond with than the man you've vowed to love forever?

Both of you can prepare for your wedding night by obtaining some information during your engagement. Kirsten, a twenty-six-year-old who has been married for several years, recommends that couples read books about sex, individually and together. "A good manual, with lots of factual information, can help both partners," she says. Couples also need to talk openly ahead of time about their expectations and attitudes.

About the honeymoon, Lori advises, "Communicate! Even on your honeymoon you're establishing patterns for the rest of your marriage. Why not take your wedding bouquet along with you to smell fresh flowers in the room? And take candles for romantic evenings. Remember, don't set unrealistically high expectations. Sex only gets better after the honeymoon." And as you pack your luggage for your honeymoon, don't forget to bring along an adventurous, tender, and tolerant attitude as well.

"You're with your best friend," says Kelly who married Kirk a year ago. "So if you're tired, you're tired. Relax together. Enjoy one another." Jamie, recently married, adds, "Don't get too hung up on achieving perfection. It's natural to be a little apprehensive. Forget about making it perfect, and just have fun."

A honeymoon is a time to create warm memories—the beginning of a lifetime of physical, emotional, and spiritual intimacy. As Benjamin Constant de Rebeque, an eighteenth century French writer and politician, once wrote: "Love makes up for the lack of long memories by a sort of magic. All other affections need a past: love creates a past which envelops us, as if by enchantment."[4]

So let your relationship create its own magic.

Chapter Eleven

THE GRAND FINALE

Today, I will marry my friend.

Five o'clock in the morning. Darkness envelopes the bedroom in my parents' old farmhouse as memories of mornings past wash over me. My stomach knots with anxiety and excitement. As I get up and head sleepily toward the bathroom, I wonder how I will feel being transformed into a bride.

Soon Yum, my soft-spoken hair stylist, arrives. Just being in her presence makes me peaceful. She bustles in, armed with industrial-strength hair spray, rollers, hairdryers, and bobby pins galore. We set up shop in the cramped, downstairs bathroom, and she begins her magic. As she styles my hair into a classic, smooth chignon, I feel elegant and bridelike, despite my red robe and furry, purple slippers.

I pause and look around at the mounds of wedding presents, the flowers, the food for my dad's sixtieth birthday party to be celebrated tonight. Our chaotic house is filled with love. Dad nervously practices his reception prayer, writing and rewriting his words of blessing, trying to capture all he wants to say.

My mom, weary from late-night phone calls and wedding details, cheerfully fastens her own wedding pearls around my neck, while my sister, clad in a long crimson dress, lifts my train ever so carefully and smiles as she straightens my veil. We have certainly had our trials and tensions over the past eight months, but today is a day of celebration and great joy.

KRISTEN

Have a Glorious Wedding Day

Your wedding day. At long last, the day you marry your best friend. How do you feel? Tired? Nervous? Quietly or deliriously happy? No matter what you feel, excitement and adrenaline will carry you through this day. As the day dawns that you and your families have spent months preparing for, remember to thank God for the gift of marriage and His gift of love. What a privilege to be able to pledge a lifetime of fidelity to the man you love. What an adventure.

❦

Now is the time to breathe deeply and to determine that, no matter what happens, you will enjoy this day. How can you have the day you have dreamed of?

Relax!

First, as you wake up, spend some quiet moments relaxing and focusing on the present, the here and now. Let go of your anxieties, recognizing that you are not responsible for glitches in the ceremony or reception, nor are you responsible for others' enjoyment of the day. Your job? To be a bride whose thoughts and senses are attuned to her groom. And after the ceremony, you and your groom can welcome all who have come to celebrate your special day.

Understand that most brides are extremely nervous in those moments before they marry. Even Lauren Bacall succumbed to a colossal case of nerves as she was about to marry Humphrey Bogart. The more anxious she grew, the more she fled to the bathroom. And when the processional began, she headed back once again. The music played on, but no one appeared. Her anxious groom called up the stairs of the Ohio farmhouse to see what had become of his bride. A disembodied voice responded from the second floor, loud enough for all the wedding guests to hear, "She's in the can!"[1]

137

Enjoy Yourself

Once you've calmed your nerves, concentrate on enjoying this special day. Your wedding, after all, lasts but a few hours. Some brides wake up the morning after the wedding somewhat sad that all too soon the wedding and reception were over, all too soon they braved the cascading rice to leave for the honeymoon. So savor each golden moment.

Don't forget to look for the touching and humorous. Though the ceremony itself is a serious and sacred event, the reception is meant to be fun and free spirited. This is the time to greet your guests, give special toasts, and laugh together. One bridesmaid even brought a catcher's mitt to the reception to increase her chances of catching the bouquet, which she did amid gales of laughter.

Forget about Making Everyone Happy

Maintaining a sense of humor will also help you deal with the people who share your day: the difficult relatives, even the divorced parents. Remember, it's not your responsibility to make others happy on this day. You can't control what guests or parents say or do. Try to be somewhat detached and bemused. And if family relationships are less than ideal, concentrate on your vows, your groom, and the spiritual significance of the day. Take the high road and allow your mother or father, or even a friend, to run interference for you.

If you and your groom have had some time alone together the previous day, it will put you in a better frame of mind. You and your fiancé may also choose to spend some final hours with a brother or sister, close friends, or a parent. One bride and her sister spent the night before the wedding, whispering and laughing until they finally fell asleep in the oak twin beds they had occupied as little girls. Another bride, Julie, spent the final hours before her wedding dressing and applying makeup, surrounded by her closest friends. As they passed around nail polish and lipstick, the young women reminisced about years past. Amy was touched by her few moments alone with her father before the ceremony. Arriving

Remember that your guests haven't come to see a flawless performance but rather to experience a real wedding of real people who love each other passionately.

❧

at the church together, they went immediately into the parlor where he nervously practiced lifting her veil, gently kissing her on the cheek, and speaking his all-important lines. Looking in her dad's weathered but loving face, she could feel his desire to support her on her day.

Forget Perfection

Most of all, forget perfection. Mishaps will occur. Expect them and choose to ignore them. At one elegant southern wedding, a tall, athletic woman who read the scripture fell headlong down the uncarpeted stairs as she left the altar. Miked, she hit the floor at the front of the stately old church with a resounding thud. Guests gasped as she lay there. Finally her escort rose from his pew and reached down to help her to her feet. The bride, who stood waiting to speak her vows, later said, "It didn't even faze me."

At another wedding the candles in the twin candelabra at the front of the church began teetering back and forth dangerously. The soloist, who sat clutching his guitar, peered through the candelabrum on the left like a Cistercian monk through a monastery grille. Guests watched as he visibly debated what to do. After a few minutes, he rose and painstakingly straightened the candles directly in front of him, only to have them again list dangerously the moment he sat down. Guests suppressed giggles at the look of consternation on the poor man's face. Meanwhile, the bride's mother, a renowned perfectionist, stared straight ahead as she anxiously waited for her daughter to appear, oblivious to this little drama.

If you're worried about potential embarrassments, just remember that your guests haven't come to see a flawless performance but rather to experience a real wedding of real people who love each other passionately. The glitches, if they occur, only add that important human touch which makes any wedding more memorable.

Third Graders Speak Out

At this point, especially if you're reading or rereading this final chapter just before your wedding day, you probably need some lighthearted advice for a happy marriage. While Debi Dietz Crawford, a third-grade teacher, was away on her honeymoon, her students,

along with a substitute teacher, decided to give her tips on how to have a lifetime of wedded bliss. We pass along their sage advice to you.

According to these wise and sometimes humorous third-graders:

"My advice for a happy marriage is if someone wants to use something of the other person's, let them use it. Don't let it become a fight."

"You should have two kids. Four is too many."

"Take turns doing the chores."

"I recommend that when you get into a fight, end it being friends."

"Take the smallest cookie."

"Go places together, like go out to dinner."

"Mostly say yes. But if you see you are going to have hot dogs for dinner and you really don't like hot dogs, it is okay to say so."

"Try not to get a divorce."

"Be wealthy."

"Stay lovers for the rest of your lives."

"Do not marry another person."

Determine that, no matter what happens,

you will enjoy this day.

❦

"Take breaks from each other once in a while."

"If there are two cupcakes and the man takes the one with not as much frosting, he loves you."

"You need to kiss every once in a while."

"Sleep together."

"Have a lot of fun."[2]

William Butler Yeats, the Irish poet and dramatist, said it well: "Hearts are not had as a gift, but hearts are earned." The trust and fidelity given to you the day you marry needs to be highly esteemed and preserved at all costs. Remember to nurture and work hard at preserving good feelings and romance in your marriage. As you walk out of the church, or home, or garden on that day of days, entrust your future to God's care. And if you're too

overwhelmed to even think two consecutive thoughts, ask your father or mother to pray for your future.

On that sunny September morning as I sat in the pew designated for the mother of the bride, I stared at the cross on the wall behind the altar and prayed, "Lord, let this be a beautiful, moving experience for Kristen and Greg. Let all who come feel the warmth of Your presence." I thought of all the prayers that had gone into this moment and the emotional and spiritual preparation Kristen and Greg had made for this day. They were ready. But was I? Was I ready to let my baby go? As Don and Kristen came down the aisle, I held my breath. My daughter had become a lovely bride, her face barely visible underneath the transparent blusher veil.

Then my close friend Kristie sang Twila Paris's "How Beautiful," and I felt my heart expand. "How beautiful the radiant bride who waits for her groom with his light in her eyes." Kristen was that radiant bride, and I, who knew her heart, understood how much this man and this woman desired to honor God on their wedding day. Would He honor them with His presence? Sunlight streamed in the windows, and I noticed that Kristen's bouquet was moving nervously from side to side. She's scared, I thought. I prayed again, and soon her shaking stopped.

As the minister intoned those ancient words, forever yoking a man and woman, I reached over and took my husband's hand. In the hush I sensed the holiness of the moment. The Lord was with us.

Marriage. God's gift to us. All too soon it was over and Kristen was now a wife. Beside her stood the young man I had grown to love. Before them stood a lifetime. And I thought of those wonderful lines from Robert Browning's "Rabbi Ben Ezra":

"Grow old along with me!
The best is yet to be
The last, for which the first was made."

BRENDA

CHAPTER 1: HOW DO I LOVE THEE?

1. *The Washington Post,* 5 January 1995.

2. "Dear Abby," *Columbia (South Carolina) The State,* 25 December 1994.

CHAPTER 2: YOUR GROOM: HIS SECRET NEEDS AND FEARS

1. Capitol Records.

2. "Engaging Proposals," *Bride's,* August/September 1993, 77.

3. George Gilder, *Men and Marriage* (Gretna, La.: Pelican Publishing Co., 1987), 47.

4. Dr. Alvin Baraff, "His Secret Fears (and Desires)," *Bride's,* April/May 1994, 122.

5. Ibid.

6. John Gray, Ph.D., *Men Are from Mars, Women Are from Venus* (New York: Harper Collins Publishers, 1992), 31.

7. Ibid., 106.

8. Mike Harden, "When Life Throws a Hardball," *Reader's Digest,* June 1995, 91–94.

9. Ibid.

10. Baraff, "His Secret Fears," 175.

11. Faye Crosby, *Juggling* (New York: The Free Press, 1991), 166.

12. Ibid.

13. Editors of *Bride's, Wedding Nightmares* (New York: Condé Nast Publishers, 1993), 54.

CHAPTER 3: WHOSE WEDDING IS IT ANYWAY?

1. Sally Friedman, "A Mother's Confessions," *Bride's,* February/March 1994, 568.

2. Ibid.

CHAPTER 4: THE FATHER OF THE BRIDE

1. John E. Brown III, "Fathers and Daughters," in *What Makes a Man?* (Colorado Springs, Colo.: NavPress, 1992), 87–88.

2. Steve Brown, "Fathers and Daughters," in *What Makes a Man?* 90.

3. Ibid., 93–94.

CHAPTER 5: THE INVISIBLE ONES: THE PARENTS OF THE GROOM

1. Erma Bombeck, "Happy Together," *Bride's,* April/May 1994, 202.

2. Ibid.

3. Deirdre Martin, "'Losing' a Son," *Bride's,* August/September 1993, 360.

4. Claire Berman, "A Daughter-in-law Gained," *Bride's,* June/July 1993, 52.

5. Brenda Hunter, *In the Company of Women* (Sisters, Ore.: Questar Publishers, 1994), 201–04.

CHAPTER 6: AMONG SISTERS AND FRIENDS

1. Editors of *Bride's, Wedding Nightmares,* 8–9.

2. Toni A. H. McNaron, ed., *The Sister Bond: A Feminist*

View of a Timeless Connection (New York: Perga-
mon Press, 1985), 7.

3. Joel Block, *Friendship: How to Give It, How to Get
It* (New York: Collier, 1980), 38.

4. Judith Martin, *Miss Manners' Guide to Excruciatingly
Correct Behavior* (London: Hamish Hamilton, 1983),
349.

CHAPTER 7: THE MEANING OF MONEY

1. Roxanne Roberts, "With This Ring I Thee Wet,"
The Washington Post, 31 July 1994.

2. *USA Today,* 1 May 1995.

3. "Estimated Costs for a Traditional Wedding in U.S.
Regions," *Bride's,* February/March 1995, 586.

CHAPTER 8: LOVE'S MASTERPIECE: YOUR WEDDING

1. Kathleen Shwar, "Musical Lore," *Bride's,*
August/September 1993, 260.

2. Jeffrey Rasche, "Scripture Ideas," *Bride's,*
December/January, 1994–1995, 364.

CHAPTER 9: CREATING A LOVE THAT LASTS

1. Lois Romano, "The Reliable Source," *The Washington
Post,* 14 February 1995, B3.

2. Elizabeth Gleick, "Should This Marriage Be Saved?"
Time, 27 February 1995, 50.

3. *The Washington Times,* 1 March 1995.

4. Gleick, "Should This Marriage Be Saved?" 50.

5. Ibid.

6. Marianne Hering, "Believe Well, Live Well," *Focus
on the Family,* September 1994, 4.

7. Ibid.

8. Ibid.

9. Ibid., 3.

CHAPTER 10: SAVING THE BEST FOR LAST

1. Dennis and Barbara Rainey, *Building Your Mate's
Self-Esteem* (San Bernardino, Cal.: Here's Life Publishers, 1986), 96.

2. *Love: Quotations from the Heart* (Philadelphia, Pa.:
Running Press, 1990).

3. Bettijane Levine, "Lovers' Nuptial Night," *The
Washington Post,* 25 March 1993.

4. *Love: Quotations from the Heart.*

CHAPTER 11: THE GRAND FINALE

1. Editors of *Bride's, Wedding Nightmares,* 7.

2. "Ann Landers," *The Washington Post,* 29 March 1995.